Centerville Library
Washington-Centerville Public Library
Centerville, Ohio

DISCARD

W9-CKT-496

THE TREE BOOK

For Kids and Their Grown-ups

Written and Illustrated by

Gina Ingoglia, ASLA

water damage to first page
made prior to 11-12-23 noted by DKC

For Davey and Lily

Elizabeth Peters
EDITOR

Steven Clemants
Gerry Moore
SCIENCE EDITORS

Patricia Hulse
EDUCATION
EDITOR

Joni Blackburn
COPY EDITOR

Elizabeth Ennis
ART DIRECTOR

Noreen Bradley
VICE-PRESIDENT
OF MARKETING

Scot Medbury
PRESIDENT

Elizabeth Scholtz
DIRECTOR
EMERITUS

Published by Brooklyn Botanic Garden, Inc.
1000 Washington Avenue, Brooklyn, NY 11215

ISBN 13: 978-1-889538-43-3
ISBN 10: 1-889538-43-4

Copyright © 2008 by Brooklyn Botanic Garden, Inc.

Printed by OGP in China.

Printed on 100% post-consumer waste recycled paper.

THANK YOU

This book took me a long, long time to finish. In fact, the reason it's finished now is because of my grandson, Davey. Whenever he saw me, he would always ask, "Is the tree book done yet?"

So my biggest thanks go to Davey.

There are also some grown-ups I'd like to thank. The first one is Dr. Bruce Hamilton (but everybody calls him "Doc"). For many years, Doc taught landscape architecture classes at Rutgers University in New Jersey. He is a teacher who taught me about trees in the first place. So a very big thanks to Doc for sharing his love of trees and for taking the time to read my manuscript and look at my drawings.

My gratitude to three presidents (past and present) of Brooklyn Botanic Garden: Donald Moore, who began this endeavor when he asked that I create this book; Judith Zuk, who will always be a part of the Garden in spirit, and who not only cheered me on but saw to it that I had a working space at the Garden so I could be near the trees; and Scot Medbury, for his enthusiasm and interest in seeing this project through.

Many other people at Brooklyn Botanic Garden have given me valuable help: My thanks to the entire publications team, including Elizabeth Peters, director of Publications and my very capable editor; Noreen Bradley, vice president of Marketing; Dr. Steven Clemants, vice president of Science; and a lovely man who is no longer with us: Dr. Stephen K-M. Tim, past vice president of Science, who carefully reviewed the manuscript and sketches. Last, but certainly not least, I especially want to thank Jackie Fazio, former director of Horticulture, who often showed me with her ever-present good nature just where to find the tree that I needed to paint.

Huge thank yous and love to my super family for having always, always, encouraged me in my work—Frank and Danis Gerdes Ingoglia, my mother and dad, who are both alive in my heart; my daughter, Melissa; my son, Barr; my son-in-law, Bill FitzPatrick; and Earl Weiner, my college sweetheart and husband, always in my corner, as I am for him.

I'm sure, like Davey, many people wondered if the tree book would ever be finished. But here it is, at last. And now Davey has someone to read it to—his little sister, Lily.

Contents

TREES

GETTING TO KNOW TREES

It's good to know about trees. The are all around us and important to us in so many ways. When you look out a window, you'll probably see a tree. They're found along busy city streets and beside quiet country roads. They grow wild in forests, and people plant them in their own backyards. The first part of this book is about trees in general—their structure, how they grow and reproduce, and other interesting facts. The second part will help you to identify and learn about different kinds of trees found in North America. You should be able to find many of them around your neighborhood or in a botanic garden or **arboretum**.

Most of the trees in this book are **native** to North America. That means that they grow naturally in the United States and were not first brought into the country from another land. A few of the trees are native to other parts of the world but are now very common in the United States.

Every tree has at least two names—a **common name** and a **scientific name**. Common names are easy to learn and remember, like paper birch. Some trees have more than one common name: For example, *paper birch* is also called *canoe birch* and *white birch*.

To avoid confusion, each kind of tree has just one scientific name. It's in Latin, so the words may seem strange. No matter how many common names a tree may have, its scientific name is always the same, all over the world. The Latin name for paper birch is *Betula papyrifera*. *Betula* means "birch" in Latin; *papyrifera* means "paper-bearing."

How tall do trees grow? Why do some trees have flat **leaves** and others have **needles**? Do all trees have **flowers** and **fruits**?

After you read this book, you'll know!

> Throughout this book, words in **bold type** are defined in the glossary starting on page 90.

HOW DOES A TREE "EAT AND DRINK"?

Animals, people, and plants can't live without food and water. Many wild animals and birds travel miles for something to eat or drink. Your family can go to a store for milk, bread, and vegetables. If you need a drink of water, you can turn on a faucet or pump water from a well. But plants, including trees, which are the largest plants of all, can't go to the supermarket or walk around looking for water. All their food and water has to be found in the soil and air right around them.

Trees get water from the soil. This water comes from rain and from underground reserves called **groundwater**. A large tree takes in hundreds of gallons of water in just one day. The water travels up the tree inside its main **stem**, which is called the **trunk.**

The water travels toward the tree through its underground **roots**. A large root called the **taproot** grows straight down. Other roots are long and reach out far from the tree trunk. Roots may grow very thick and help hold the tree to the ground. But only the fine **root hairs** at the ends of all the roots take the water from the soil.

Inside the roots, the tree changes the water into a liquid called **root sap**. The root sap moves up the tree trunk in a layer of wood called the **sapwood** or **xylem**. Inside the xylem, the root sap travels through the branches and out to the **leaves**. This is how water gets inside all parts of the tree. Dissolved in the water are **minerals** and **salts** from the soil. Trees need minerals and salts to grow, like you need your daily vitamins.

Leaves make food for the tree. They do this with light from the sun and a special green substance called **chlorophyll**. Chlorophyll gives the leaves their green color. With sunlight and chlorophyll, the leaves change moisture and gases from the air into a kind of food called **sugars**. This process is called **photosynthesis**. The sugars feed the tree by moving from the leaves all through the branches and down to the roots. The sugars move right beneath the **bark** in a layer of wood called the **bast** or **phloem**.

If a tree gets enough food and water, it grows. Different types of trees grow at different speeds and to different heights. When a tree is **mature** it won't grow taller, but it still grows new leaves and wood.

In the fall, in places where the weather gets cold, some trees slow down. The days are short and there isn't enough sunlight for leaves to make many sugars. In icy winter, roots can't take in water that's frozen in the ground. Some trees drop off their leaves and take a break from making a lot of food by photosynthesis. (These types of trees are called **deciduous** trees.)

In springtime, the weather gets warm and the days have more hours of sunshine. Spring rains soak the ground around the tree. Thawed root sap rises up the trunk and out to the branches. **Buds** open and new leaves and **flowers** appear. The tree is "eating and drinking" again.

BETTER BELEAF IT!

Every kind of tree has its own kind of **leaf**. Some full-grown leaves are tinier than your pinkie fingernail. Others grow as big as umbrellas. Leaf edges are wavy, smooth, or **serrated** (toothed like a saw). Their surfaces might be waxy or hairy. Delicate leaves, thin as paper, tear easily. Tougher leaves are thicker, and many feel like leather.

Many trees lose their leaves during part of the year. These kinds of trees are called **deciduous** trees. Trees that keep most of their leaves, like pines and spruces, are called **evergreen** trees.

Leaf Buds

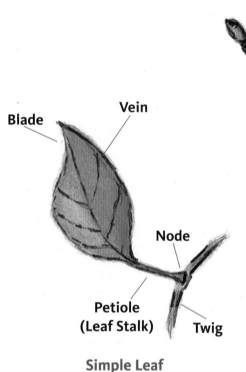

Blade — Vein — Node — Petiole (Leaf Stalk) — Twig

Simple Leaf

Leaflet

Compound Leaf

Each kind of tree has its own **leaf bud**. Look for them on the bare branches in winter. In spring, the buds begin to grow, and then new leaves appear.

The flat, broad part of a leaf is the **blade**. A leaf with one blade is called a **simple leaf**. The "lines" that you often see on leaves are called **veins**. The blade is often attached to the branch by a **leaf stalk** or **petiole**.

The blades of some leaves are divided into **leaflets**. These leaflets may look like many leaves, but they're really parts of only one leaf. This kind of leaf is called a **compound leaf**.

Leaves are attached to the **twig** in one of three ways. They may be **opposite** one another or arranged in an **alternate**, staggered pattern. Three or more leaves attached in a ring around the twig are called **whorled**. Most trees have alternate leaves. To remember four trees with opposite leaves, just say **MAD HORSE**—**M**aple, **A**sh, **D**ogwood, **Horse** chestnut!

Opposite   **Alternate**   **Whorled**

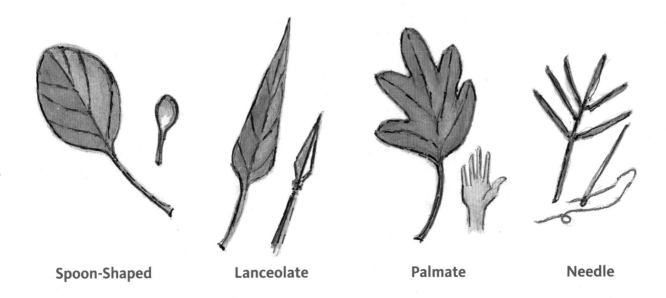

Spoon-Shaped **Lanceolate** **Palmate** **Needle**

Leaves are also named after their shape. Some are **spoon-shaped**. **Lanceolate** leaves are pointed like sharp lances or spears. A leaf shaped like a hand with four fingers and a thumb is called **palmate**—named after the palm of your hand. Thin evergreen leaves, like those that grow on pine trees, are called **needles**.

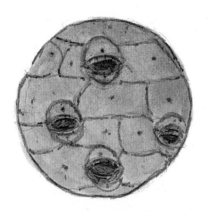

Stomata (Magnified)

If you study a leaf under a microscope, you'll see tiny openings. Each opening is called a **stoma**. Stomata (which is what you call more than one stoma) are usually on the underside of a leaf. When the stomata are open, the leaf can take in and give off gases and moisture. People breathe in a gas called **oxygen** from the air. Our bodies use up the oxygen and breathe out a gas we don't need called **carbon dioxide**. Trees breathe in oxygen too. But mostly they do just the opposite: When they perform **photosynthesis**, trees take in carbon dioxide and give off oxygen—more oxygen than they use, so there's some left over for us to breathe. That's why it's healthy for us to have lots of trees around.

So the next time you look at a leaf, you'll know if it's simple or compound, alternate or opposite, lanceolate or palmate. And where's the petiole?

HOW LEAVES CHANGE COLOR

Ginkgo

White Oak

It's fall. Summer vacation is over and you are back in school. The cool air makes you feel full of energy and ready for a long, busy winter.

It's the opposite with most **deciduous** trees. They slow down in the fall. Their **leaves** change color and drop to the ground. During the winter their branches are bare. It's hard to tell if some trees are even alive.

Trees grow all spring and summer. Their leaves look green because they contain green **pigments** called **chlorophyll**. The chlorophyll uses sunlight to change water and gases from the air into food for the tree. Leaves also contain yellow and orange pigments. They are called **carotenoids**. Carotenoids are there in the leaves all summer. But you can't see them because there are so many chlorophyll pigments. They cover up the carotenoids.

The fall weather is too cold for the chlorophyll to work properly. It breaks up and disappears. But the carotenoids stay behind. Now the leaves are yellow. Some trees with yellow fall color are ginkgos, honey locusts, and tulip trees.

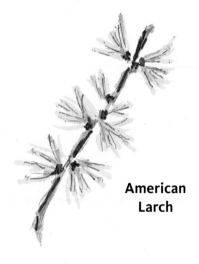

American Larch

Tupelo

Flowering Dogwood

Paper Birch

Sugar Maple

What about the leaves that turn pink, red, or purple? These colors come from pigments called **anthocyanins**. These pigments aren't in the leaves all summer long. Anthocyanins are made in the leaf in the fall. Their colors are brightest when the weather is just right. The days must be sunny and not too hot or cold. The nights must be very cold but not freezing.

Sugar maples have bright red fall color. Their leaves make lots of anthocyanin pigments.

If you're painting a picture and mix some colors together, you get new colors. It's the same with leaves. The combinations of their pigments create many colors.

But remember, each kind of tree has its own mixture of pigments. That's why a ginkgo leaf always turns yellow but never red!

Honey Locust

Shagbark Hickory

Sweetgum

WHICH COMES FIRST: FLOWERS OR FRUIT?

Trees grow from **seeds**. The seeds grew inside a **fruit**. And fruits come from **flowers**. It may sound complicated, but it really isn't.

Tree flowers grow in different shapes and sizes. A magnolia **blossom** may be bigger than your hand. Oak and maple flowers are so tiny you might not notice them. Lots of trees bloom in the springtime. But bright yellow golden-rain tree flowers don't appear until late summer.

There are **male flowers, female flowers**, and **perfect flowers.**

A male flower produces **pollen**, which looks like dust. A female flower contains an **ovary**, which is like a tiny egg-shaped container. Seeds grow inside the ovary. A perfect flower has both pollen and an ovary.

The Parts of a Perfect Flower

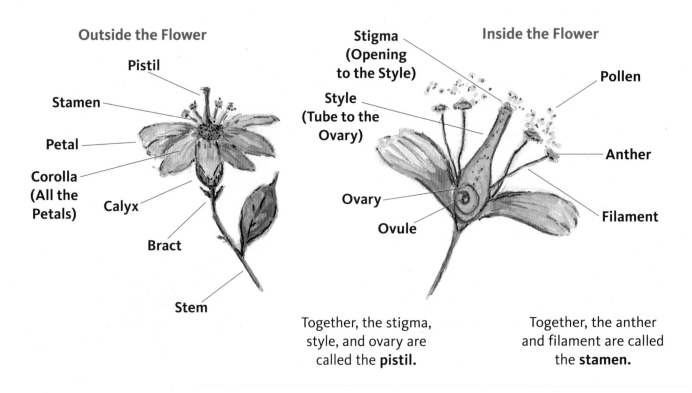

Together, the stigma, style, and ovary are called the **pistil.**

Together, the anther and filament are called the **stamen.**

To make a fruit, some pollen has to make its way to the ovary at just the right time. This is called **pollination**. The wind often helps with pollination by blowing pollen from flower to flower. Bees also help when they land on flowers to sip sweet juices called **nectar** and to gather pollen to make honey. They store the pollen in little sacs on their legs. Then they take it back to the hive. While a bee is collecting pollen or sipping nectar, it may brush some pollen against a flower's **stigma**. If this happens when the flower's ovary is **mature**, the pollen might **fertilize** it. After a flower is fertilized, the seed begins to grow. To protect the seed, a fruit grows around it.

There are two kinds of fruits: **fleshy fruits** and **dry fruits**.

Fleshy fruits, such as apples and peaches, are soft and juicy, and people and other animals like to eat some kinds of them. A peach contains one large seed called a **pit**. When you cut an apple in half, you can see its seeds around the core. When fleshy fruits are ripe, they drop to the ground.

Fleshy Fruits

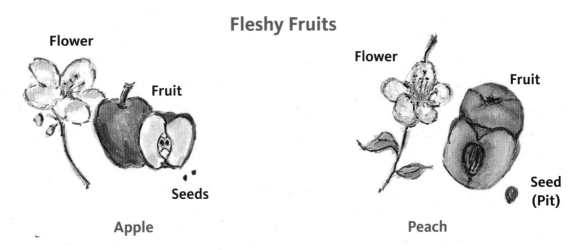

Flower

Fruit

Seeds

Apple

Flower

Fruit

Seed (Pit)

Peach

Most of the fruits in this book are dry fruits. Dry fruits are hard. The seeds are protected inside **pods** or **shells**. Some dry fruits, like **nuts**, are eaten by people. Many kinds are eaten by animals. **Acorns**, which grow on oak trees, are dry fruits. Squirrels often bury acorns to eat later. But if they don't dig them up, an acorn may sprout and become a tall oak.

Dry Fruits

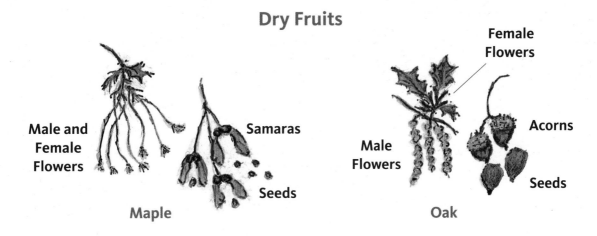

Male and Female Flowers

Samaras

Seeds

Maple

Female Flowers

Male Flowers

Acorns

Seeds

Oak

Some dry fruits are so light they float on the wind. A maple tree fruit is called a **samara**. On papery wings, spinning like helicopters, samaras can carry their tiny seeds far from the tree.

A prickly dry fruit might get stuck in an animal's fur. As the animal wanders from place to place, it carries the fruit with it. When the fruit finally drops off, its seed may sprout.

Birds also spread seeds. They might swallow a fruit and fly away. When the seed passes from the bird's body, it may land miles from where the fruit was eaten.

If a seed lands on the ground and it gets enough light and water, it sends down tiny **roots**. Then a little tree, called a **seedling**, starts to grow.

WHAT GOES ON INSIDE A CONE

Conifers, which are mostly evergreen trees, have **leaves** that are shaped like needles. They grow on small branches called **branchlets**. Most conifers keep their **needles** all year long—even where the winters are very cold.

Instead of having **flowers** and **fruits**, conifers have **pollen cones** and **seed cones**. On many conifers, the pollen cones and young seed cones are tiny. You may not notice them unless you look very carefully. Each conifer has its own kind of cone. The cones on this page are from the eastern white pine tree.

Pollen Cones

Immature Seed Cones

In springtime, the pollen cones release **pollen** into the air. Sometimes there's so much pollen it looks like clouds of yellow dust. Some of it may land inside a seed cone. At first, the seed cone often looks like a tiny ball close to the tip of a branch. This is called an **immature** cone. If pollen lands in it, the seed cone is **pollinated** and begins to grow and change shape. It's made up of tightly closed **scales** that protect the **seeds** developing inside. After the cone is fully grown, or **mature**, it dries out and the scales open.

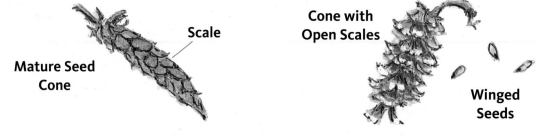

Scale

Mature Seed Cone

Cone with Open Scales

Winged Seeds

If you pull the cone apart, you can see the seeds resting on top of each scale. Each seed has a thin papery covering. It acts like a tiny wing and helps the wind carry the seeds away. **Winged seeds** may blow miles from the tree. When the seed lands on the ground, if it gets enough light and water, it **sprouts**. Roots are sent down into the soil and a new evergreen tree begins to grow.

When seed cones are fully grown, they are usually easy to see on the tree. Here's a collection of them. These trees are all in this book.

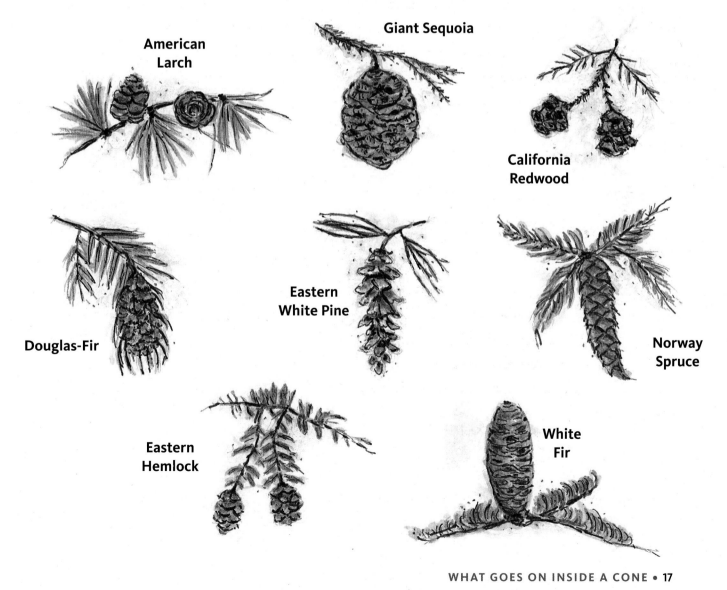

American Larch

Giant Sequoia

California Redwood

Douglas-Fir

Eastern White Pine

Norway Spruce

Eastern Hemlock

White Fir

DON'T FORGET THE BARK!

If you were asked to describe a tree, you'd probably talk about its size, the **fruit**, the **flowers**, or the shape of the **leaves**. And you might not say a word about the **bark**.

But if you take the time to look, you'll see that bark is one of the tree's most interesting parts. By just studying the bark alone, plant experts can identify a tree.

Look at the bark's color. Lots of trees have gray bark, but some barks are shades of yellow, brown, white, or red. Next, what does the bark feel like? Is it peeling? Or scaly? Grooved or smooth? Is it blocky and bumpy like an alligator's skin? Or as wrinkly as an elephant's?

Bark covers the tree like a skin. It protects the inner wood from insect damage, disease, and harsh weather. Some barks are almost as thin as a sheet of paper. Others may grow to be several inches thick.

The nice thing about bark scouting is that you can do it anytime. Fruits and flowers and leaves might not stay on the tree throughout the year—but the bark is *always* there!

Bark

It takes years for a tree's **bark** to fully develop. These drawings show bark on grown trees. The important thing to remember is that each tree has its own kind of bark.

Cherry

Saucer Magnolia

Honey Locust

London Planetree

Franklinia

Flowering Dogwood

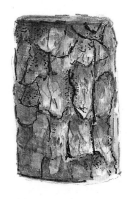

Eastern White Pine

European Beech

Weeping Willow

Mimosa Tree

Eastern Redcedar

Tupelo

THE INSIDE STORY

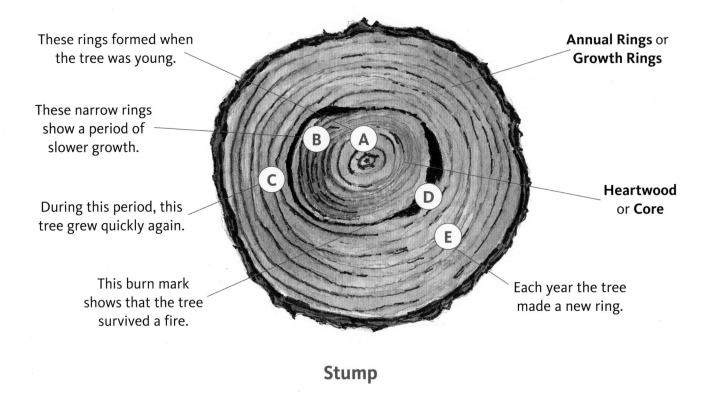

These rings formed when the tree was young.

These narrow rings show a period of slower growth.

During this period, this tree grew quickly again.

This burn mark shows that the tree survived a fire.

Annual Rings or **Growth Rings**

Heartwood or **Core**

Each year the tree made a new ring.

A B C D E

Stump

After a tree is cut down, the part of the **trunk** left standing is called the **stump**. Take a look at one. The wood in the center of the trunk is called the **heartwood** or **core**. The heartwood is the oldest wood, and it no longer conducts water. The living wood grows in layers or rings around the heartwood. The layers are called **annual rings** or **growth rings**. Each year a new ring of wood grows.

Different kinds of trees grow different-sized rings. Some are one-eighth-inch thick; others may be wider or narrower. The newest and largest ring is closest to the **bark**. The oldest and smallest ring is in the core. If you count the rings, you get a pretty fair idea of the tree's age when it was cut down. But remember, it won't be exact. Some species of trees may grow two or more rings a year.

Some trees can live hundreds of years. Their oldest rings may have formed before Columbus sailed to America!

Look at the section of tree trunk on this page. It can reveal something about the tree when it was alive.

A. These annual rings were formed when the tree was young. They're pretty evenly spaced. The tree was growing steadily. It must have gotten enough sunlight, air, and water.

B. Now the rings are very narrow. The tree's growth had slowed down. Was it just slowing down naturally for a few years, or did something else cause this? Maybe yearly swarms of insects ate the tree's leaves and it couldn't make enough food to grow very much. Maybe there was a **drought**, which means it didn't rain and the tree didn't get much water. Without enough water, the tree's **roots** couldn't absorb **minerals** from the soil. Maybe other trees were growing close by. During these years, they'd grown tall enough to block out the tree's sunlight. Without enough sunlight, a tree can't make enough **sugars** to grow well.

    Sometimes, if conditions are very bad, a tree won't grow any rings at all. Insect attacks, lack of water, or not enough sunlight can kill a tree. But in this case, no matter what the problem, the tree was able to survive.

C. Here the tree is growing at top speed again. Perhaps the insects had stopped attacking or the drought ended. Or maybe the nearby trees were cut down or blew down in a storm.

D. This black mark was caused by a burn. That year, a forest fire damaged the tree but didn't kill it.

E. The tree added new annual rings over the burn mark. Each year, the tree continued to grow until it was cut down.

It's only after a tree dies that we can discover its past. For years, scientists have been studying trees' annual rings to find out about forest fires, climate changes, insect attacks, and other natural events. Seeing when and how often these events took place in the past may help scientists to predict what could happen in the future!

WINTER CLUES

Vase-shaped trees look
something like a container
for flowers.

Trees with a **weeping habit**
have trailing, drooping
branches.

Columnar trees grow tall
and narrow like columns.

Evergreen trees, such as firs, pines, and spruces, look the same all year long. But **deciduous** trees, such as oaks and maples, lose their **leaves** in the winter. Without leaves, when branches are bare, it's harder to recognize a type of tree. But there are some tricks to help you identify it.

Tree experts can identify trees in winter just by looking at the branching patterns. Each kind of tree has its own shape or way of growing. It's called its **habit**. Some habits are pretty easy to recognize.

If you look very carefully at the tree, you may find more clues. Take a look at the **bark**. A paper birch's bright white bark stands out even from far away. Another tree that's easy to spot is the shagbark hickory, because it has rough bark that looks different than the bark of other trees.

Sometimes dried leaves still on the trees can be clues. You can also identify trees with bare branches by looking at the **leaf buds**. They grow differently on each kind of tree.

By the end of autumn, most trees have already dropped their **fruit**, but some trees keep their fruit for much of the winter. But be careful: If you see a honey locust **pod** lying on the ground next to a tree, you can't say, "Oh, this must be a honey locust," because an animal might have dropped it there. But if you see a tree with a honey locust pod dangling from a branch, then you can be sure that it's a honey locust!

The more you learn about trees, the easier it will become for you to identify them—even in winter.

WHY DO WE NEED TREES?

Trees do a lot more than make the landscape look nice. They help us to live.

People and animals stay alive by breathing in **oxygen**—a gas that's in the air. With every breath, you take oxygen out of the air and use it inside your body. The waste gas that you breathe out is called **carbon dioxide**. Plants do the opposite when they perform **photosynthesis**. They take in carbon dioxide. Then they "breathe" out oxygen into the air.

Leaves can act like tiny air conditioners. They give off water vapor and make the air cooler on hot summer days. Leaves block out the sun and provide shade. They trap billions of dust and **pollen** specks. This cut downs on air pollution. **Roots** tie a tree to the ground to keep it from toppling over. But they also hold the soil in place. During heavy rainstorms, roots keep the ground from washing away. This helps prevent floods and landslides.

Trees can protect people and plants from wind. Farmers plant rows of trees, called **windbreaks**, next to their fields. When a strong wind blows across the land, it hits the windbreaks. The trees break up the force of the wind, protect the crops, and keep the soil from blowing away.

Trees provide us with wood. Firewood is burned for heat and sometimes for cooking. We build wooden houses and furniture—and make wooden tools, fences, railroad ties, toys, and sporting equipment. **Cellulose**, a main part of wood, is ground into pulp and manufactured into paper, suntan lotion, and shatterproof glass.

Trees provide homes for animals—squirrels, birds, frogs, bats, and insects. Bears may spend the winter hibernating inside a hollow tree.

Trees give us food—fruits, nuts, and maple syrup. For thousands of years, people have made medicines from **bark** and leaves. Today, scientists are discovering new ways trees can keep us healthy.

These are just some of the ways that trees help us. Now, do we need trees? What do *you* think?

WHITE ASH
Fraxinus americana
(**frak**-si-nus ah-**mer**-ih-**kay**-nah)

Also called
American ash

Native to eastern U.S.

Deciduous

Can grow to
120 feet tall in the wild

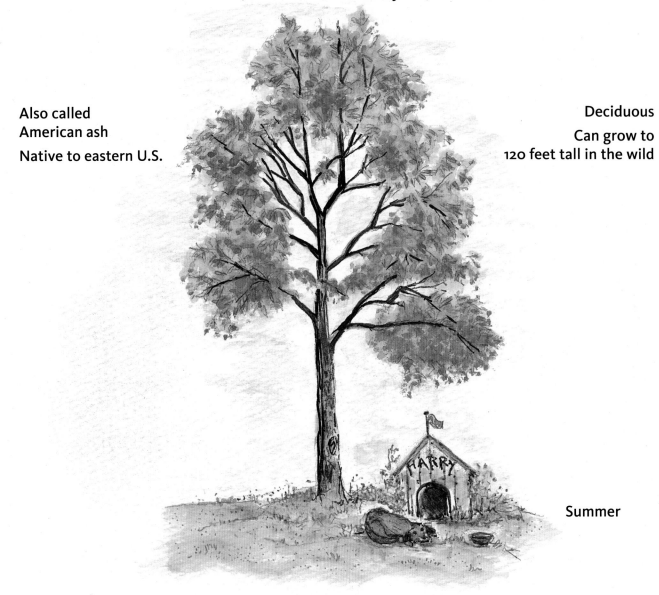

Summer

The white ash often grows in abandoned fields. When farmland isn't used anymore, trees and other plants begin to grow there. The white ash is one of the first trees to appear.

White ash grows fairly fast and can live for hundreds of years. Its wood is hard and strong. This is unusual because trees that grow fast usually have weak wood.

Its smooth, tough wood can take hard treatment and is used a lot for sports equipment—baseball bats, oars, and hockey sticks. Sturdy baskets, axe handles, and farming equipment are often made of white ash. White ash wood can also be bent by using special equipment. It's often used to make chairs with curved backs or other furniture where curved wood is needed.

George Washington, the first president of the United States, planted a white ash at Mount Vernon, his house in Virginia. It was said to be one of his favorite trees.

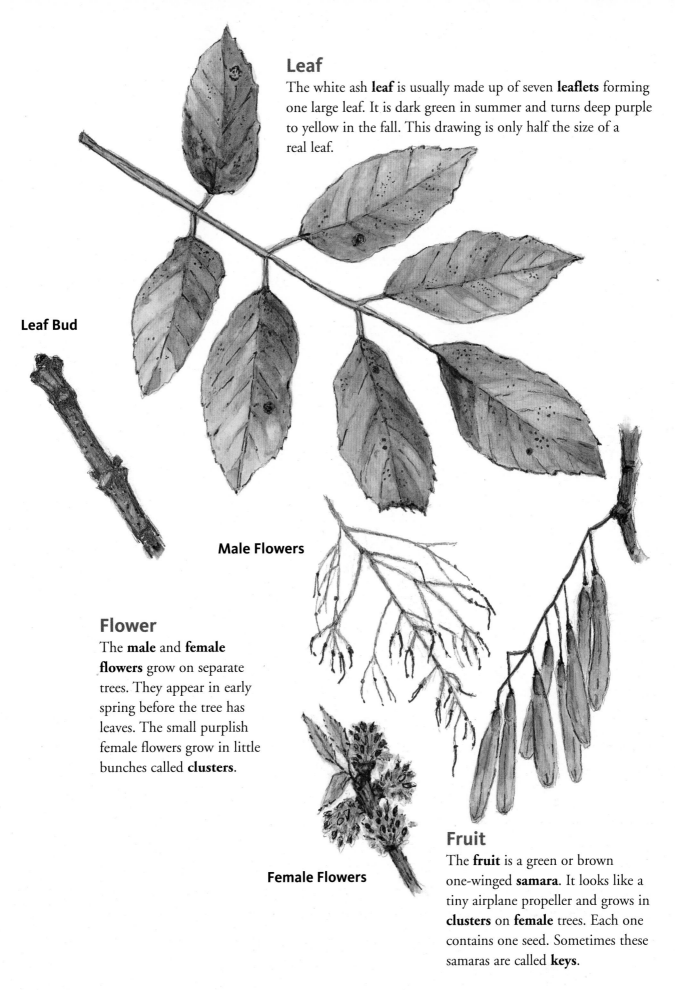

Leaf

The white ash **leaf** is usually made up of seven **leaflets** forming one large leaf. It is dark green in summer and turns deep purple to yellow in the fall. This drawing is only half the size of a real leaf.

Leaf Bud

Male Flowers

Flower

The **male** and **female flowers** grow on separate trees. They appear in early spring before the tree has leaves. The small purplish female flowers grow in little bunches called **clusters**.

Female Flowers

Fruit

The **fruit** is a green or brown one-winged **samara**. It looks like a tiny airplane propeller and grows in **clusters** on **female** trees. Each one contains one seed. Sometimes these samaras are called **keys**.

BASSWOOD
Tilia americana
(**til**-ee-ah ah-**mer**-ih-**kay**-nah)

Also called
American linden

Native to U.S.

Deciduous
60–80 feet tall

Spring

Bees make excellent honey from **flowers** that grow on the basswood tree. In the spring, the tree buzzes with the busy insects as they gather **nectar** from the pale yellow **blossoms**. For this reason the basswood is often called "the bee tree." The flowers have also been used for making a tea.

Because basswood wood has no odor or taste, it's used to make food containers, including boxes for its honey. The wood carves well. Iroquois American Indians carved false faces (masks) on the trunks of living basswoods. When the masks were finished, they cut them off the tree and hollowed them out so the false faces could be worn. They were usually painted red or black.

American Indians also made ropes from the stringy inner **bark**. In the spring, they stripped off some bark and soaked it in water for several weeks. Then they pounded the strips and twisted them into ropes. Old basswood trunks are often hollow and make good nesting places for small animals.

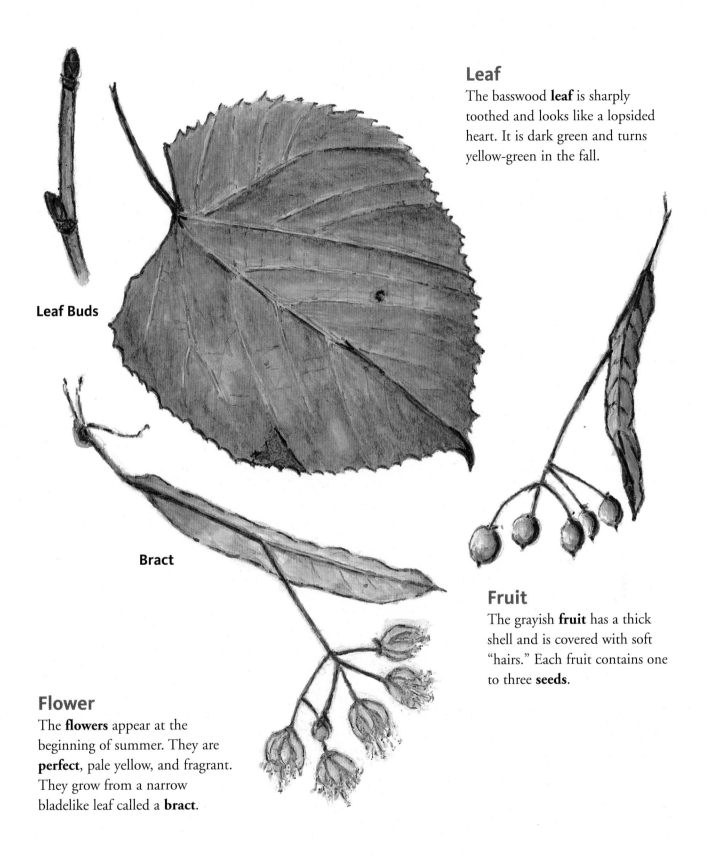

Leaf

The basswood **leaf** is sharply toothed and looks like a lopsided heart. It is dark green and turns yellow-green in the fall.

Leaf Buds

Bract

Fruit

The grayish **fruit** has a thick shell and is covered with soft "hairs." Each fruit contains one to three **seeds**.

Flower

The **flowers** appear at the beginning of summer. They are **perfect**, pale yellow, and fragrant. They grow from a narrow bladelike leaf called a **bract**.

EUROPEAN BEECH
Fagus sylvatica
(**fay**-gus sil-**vat**-ih-kah)

Native to central
and southern Europe

Deciduous
50–60 feet tall

Summer

The European beech needs lots of room to grow. It's a beautiful wide tree with branches reaching toward the ground. The **bark** is the tree's most unusual feature. It looks a lot like an elephant's hide—smooth and gray with some wrinkles and folds!

People who study history believe that some of the first books were written on smooth beech bark. The word *book* comes from another word meaning "beech."

Beech wood is strong and is an important timber tree in Europe. It's used for furniture, especially school desks and workbenches. For hundreds of years, many people slept on mattresses that they stuffed with straw. But beech leaves were also popular mattress stuffers. The leaves felt bouncier and more comfortable and lasted longer than straw.

Beech **fruit** are called beechnuts. Chipmunks and squirrels feast on millions of them each year. Some farmers feed beechnuts to their animals. Hungry pigs and turkeys gobble them right up!

Leaf Buds

Leaf

In May, when European beech **leaves** first appear, they are pale green. Then they become shiny and darker green and feel sort of hairy underneath. In the fall, the leaves turn brownish red and gold.

Female Flowers

Flower

The **male flowers** grow in tassels of **stamens** that contain **pollen** to **pollinate** female flowers. The **female flowers** look like buds. After they are pollinated, they become prickly green egg-shaped **husks** called **burs**. Burs contain beechnuts.

Male Flowers

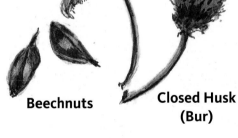

Open Husk (Bur)

Beechnuts

Closed Husk (Bur)

Fruit

Beechnuts are shiny brown and three-sided. They grow inside a prickly **husk** or **bur** that develops from the **female flower**. In the fall, the husk splits into four parts to release the beechnuts. Two or three beechnuts are in each husk.

PAPER BIRCH
Betula papyrifera
(**bet**-u-lah pap-uh-**rif**-er-ah)

Also called
canoe birch, white birch

Native to North America

Deciduous
50–70 feet tall
**State tree of
New Hampshire**

Summer

The paper birch is at home in dry places and is easy to recognize because of its chalky white **bark**. When the tree is still young, the bark is yellowish brown. As it grows, the bark turns white and, in time, develops black markings. The bark peels off the tree, uncovering a reddish-orange inner bark.

American Indians made the paper birch an important part of their lives. They ate and cooked with birch bark utensils and covered their homes with it. In the snowy north they wore birch-wood snowshoes.

Paper birch bark is waterproof. To construct lightweight canoes, the Indians stretched strips of birch bark over frames of northern white cedar wood. They sewed the strips with thread made from larch tree **roots** and sealed the seams with **resin** from pine and fir trees.

The tree sheds its bark naturally, but it should never be pulled from a live tree. When bark is stripped off, black scars are left behind. Stripping may also kill a tree. Paper birch wood is used to make ice cream sticks, toothpicks, clothespins, spools, and broom handles. Paper birch bark burns even if it's wet! This makes it handy for starting campfires.

Leaf

The paper birch **leaf** is oval-shaped and **serrated**. Its dull dark green color changes to bright yellow in the fall.

Leaf Buds

Female Catkin

Flower

Male and female flowers grow on the same tree. **Male flowers** grow in long **catkins** that are full of **pollen**. **Female flowers** grow in tiny catkins that are shaped like small cigars.

Male Catkins Ripe with Pollen

Female Catkin Developing into Fruit

Fruit

After the **female catkin** is **pollinated**, it grows into a brown papery cone shape containing tiny two-winged **nutlets** (**fruit**).

Bark

A birch's mature outer **bark** is white with black markings. Inner bark is reddish orange.

JAPANESE FLOWERING CHERRY
Prunus cultivars
(**proo**-nus **kul**-ti-varz)

Native to Asia

Deciduous

**Most cultivars:
20–35 feet tall**

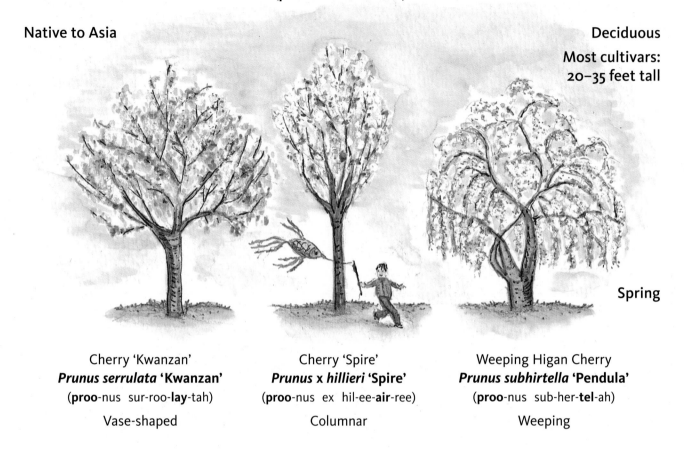

Spring

Cherry 'Kwanzan'	Cherry 'Spire'	Weeping Higan Cherry
***Prunus serrulata* 'Kwanzan'**	***Prunus* x *hillieri* 'Spire'**	***Prunus subhirtella* 'Pendula'**
(**proo**-nus sur-roo-**lay**-tah)	(**proo**-nus ex hil-ee-**air**-ree)	(**proo**-nus sub-her-**tel**-ah)
Vase-shaped	Columnar	Weeping

Japanese flowering cherries are small trees known for their **blossoms**. There are more than 120 different kinds or **cultivars**. Most of the cherry cultivars do not live much longer than 30 years. Some cultivars have pink or reddish blossoms; others have white. The flowers may grow singly (alone) or in **clusters** (little bunches). The shapes of the trees are not all the same. They may be **columnar** (narrow), **vase-shaped**, or **weeping** (drooping). Many have no **fruit** at all. If they do have some, they are small, black, and not good to eat. Inside, a hard **pit** contains the **seed**. A soft fruit with a pit is called a **drupe**. Peaches, dates, apricots, and the cherries that you can eat are also drupes.

Thousands of flowering cherries grow in Washington, DC, the nation's capital. They were given in friendship by the people of Japan. Many are planted alongside a body of water called the Tidal Basin. Every spring a cherry blossom festival is held and people from all over the world come to see them. Brooklyn Botanic Garden in New York is also famous for its Japanese flowering cherries. They too were given to the Garden by the people of Japan to show their friendship. Every spring a *sakura matsuri* (cherry blossom festival) is held at the Garden to celebrate the blooming of the trees.

Flower

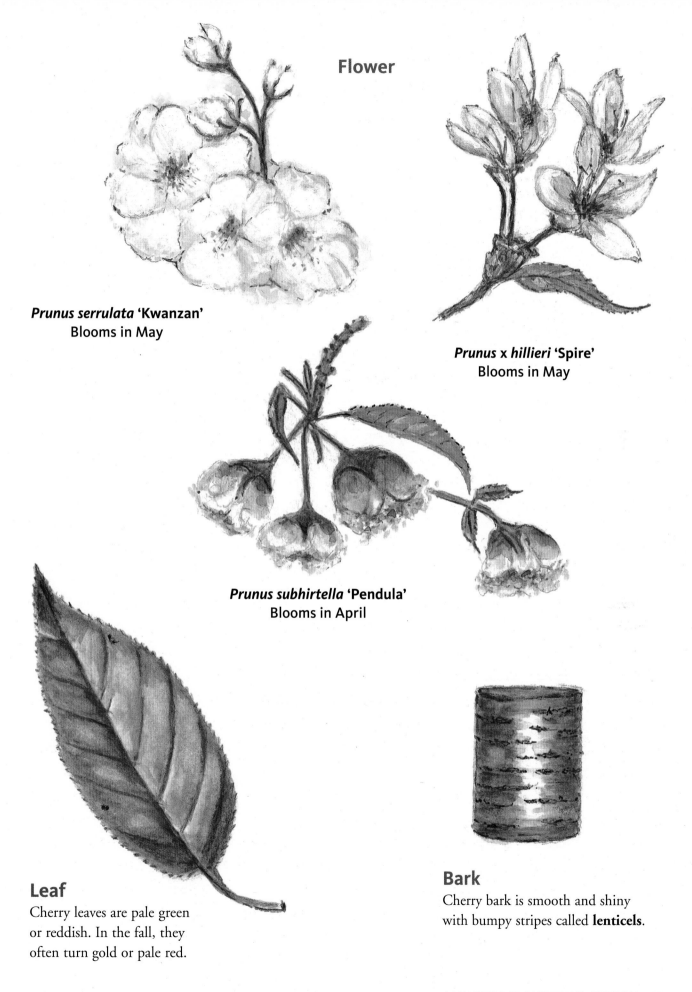

***Prunus serrulata* 'Kwanzan'**
Blooms in May

***Prunus* x *hillieri* 'Spire'**
Blooms in May

***Prunus subhirtella* 'Pendula'**
Blooms in April

Leaf
Cherry leaves are pale green
or reddish. In the fall, they
often turn gold or pale red.

Bark
Cherry bark is smooth and shiny
with bumpy stripes called **lenticels**.

FLOWERING DOGWOOD
Cornus florida
(**kor**-nus **flor**-ih-duh)

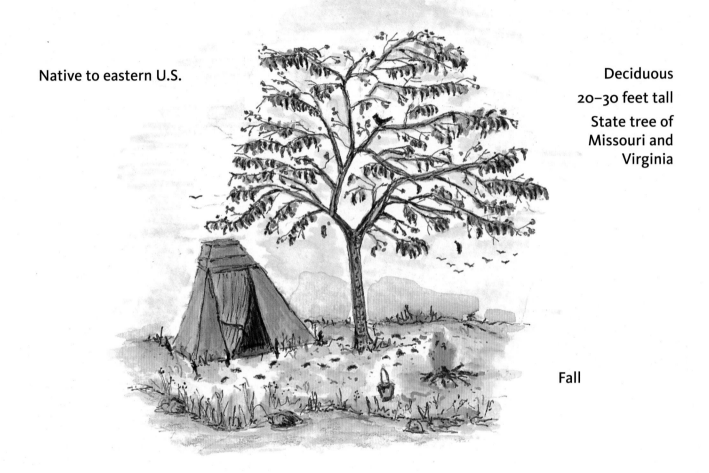

Native to eastern U.S.

Deciduous
20–30 feet tall
State tree of
Missouri and
Virginia

Fall

The flowering dogwood is a small tree that often grows in shady spots in the woods. In springtime, before most of the **leaves** begin to grow, the branches are covered with white **blooms**. In summer they are gone, but in the fall, bright red **fruit** appear in their place. They seem to be a special treat for some animals. Birds and squirrels eat most of the dogwood fruit long before winter arrives.

This tree is not named after an animal. The word *dog* has another meaning. A dog is a long pointed stick that is used in cooking over a fire. Pieces of meat, skewered on the dog, were held above the flames to cook. Hundreds of years ago, branches from this tree were used to make dogs.

Dogwood wood is heavy, hard, and tough. It's used for tool handles and golf club heads.

American Indians used the **bark** and **roots** to make medicine to treat a sickness called malaria. They made red dye from the roots. If you pound the ends of a tiny dogwood **branchlet**, you can make a sort of toothbrush. It's even supposed to make your teeth look whiter.

Leaf

The flowering dogwood **leaf** is dark green. In the fall, it turns bright red to reddish purple.

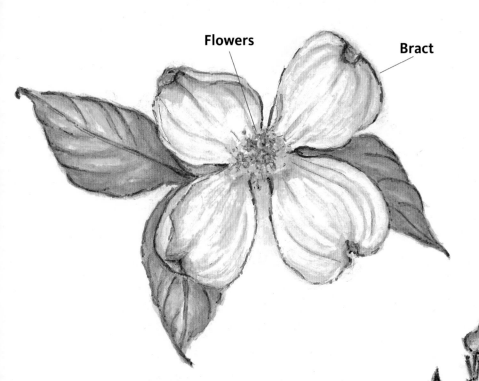

Flowers

Bract

Fruit Cluster

After the **flowers** are **pollinated**, they turn into **clusters of fruit**. The glossy red fruit are called **drupes**. The football-shaped drupes ripen during September and October.

Flower Clusters and Bracts

The blue-gray **flower bud** looks something like a helmet. In April or May, the tiny flowers grow in little **clusters** with large **bracts** that open around the base of each cluster. The white, pink-edged bracts are usually mistaken for flower **petals**.

Leaf Bud

Flower Bud

DOUGLAS-FIR
Pseudotsuga menziesii
(**soo**-do-**tsoo**-ga men-**zee**-see-eye)

Native to western
North America

Evergreen
40–350 feet tall
State tree of
Oregon

Summer

The Douglas-fir was named for a famous Scottish **botanist** and explorer named David Douglas, who lived from 1790 to 1834. This tree has a confusing name because it's not a fir at all but another type of **conifer**. In the past, the Douglas-fir had different **scientific names** when botanists thought it was related to different kinds of trees. The one you see listed above is its name today.

The Douglas-fir is one of the tallest trees in the world, second only to the huge sequoias. On the east coast of the United States, it grows to only about 40 feet tall, but on the west coast, it can reach 350 feet in height and almost 12 feet in diameter (the distance across its trunk).

The Douglas-fir is one of the world's most important timber trees. The wood is unusually strong and is used in building construction and for ladders, boxes, cabinets, and flooring. Douglas-fir helped to settle the American West: Its strong wood was used for miles of railroad ties. Because its **needles** don't fall off easily, Douglas-fir is one of the most popular Christmas trees.

Leaf

The Douglas-fir has flat **needles**. They may be green, gray-green, or bluish. Pointed buds grow on the ends of the branches.

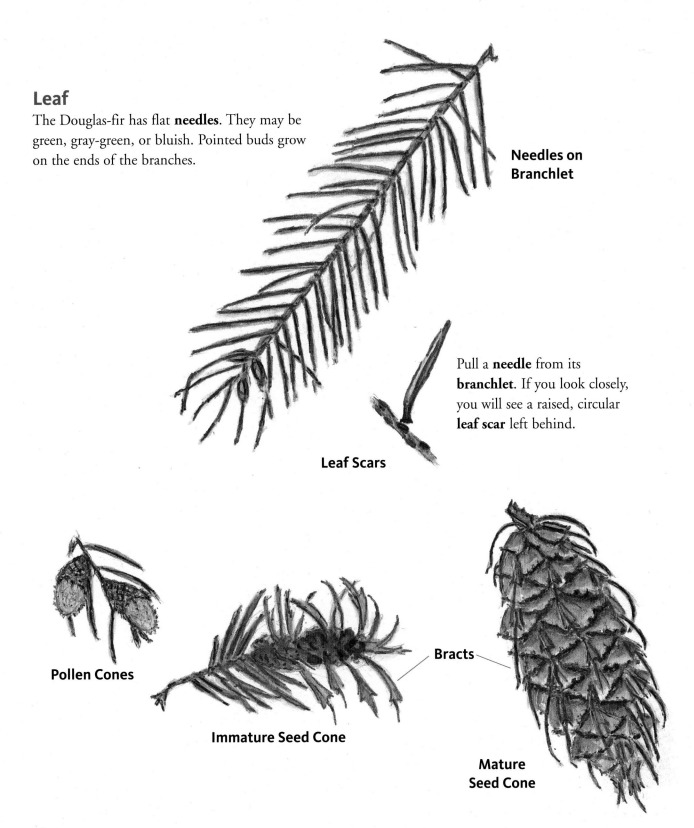

Needles on Branchlet

Pull a **needle** from its **branchlet**. If you look closely, you will see a raised, circular **leaf scar** left behind.

Leaf Scars

Pollen Cones

Immature Seed Cone

Bracts

Mature Seed Cone

Cone

The **pollen (male) cones** are very small. The pretty **seed (female) cones** are larger and reddish purple with long, three-pointed **bracts**. After the seed cone is **pollinated** and grows to its full size, the papery bracts can be easily seen hanging below the **scales**. A Douglas-fir cone always hangs downward, and it stays on the tree far into winter.

AMERICAN ELM
Ulmus americana
(**ul**-mus ah-**mer**-ih-**kay**-nuh)

Also called
white elm, gray elm,
water elm, swamp elm
Native to eastern U.S.

Deciduous
60–80 feet tall
State tree of
North Dakota and
Massachusetts

Summer

The American elm was once one of the best-known trees in the United States. Its **vase-shaped habit** was a familiar sight in towns and cities across the country. When these elms were planted on opposite sides of the street, their branches formed graceful arches of green.

Today, most of these magnificent trees are no longer alive. Thousands have been killed by Dutch elm disease. This disease is spread mostly by infected bark beetles. The cause of the disease was discovered by Dutch scientists, and that's how the disease got its name. Many cities are trying to save their American elms, but no cure for the disease has been found.

Dutch elm disease was brought to the United States around 1930. It came in from another country in a shipment of logs to New England. The wood contained some infected beetles, and these insects began the spread of the disease. The sad story of the American elm teaches us all an important lesson: All foreign plant material must be carefully inspected before it can come into this country.

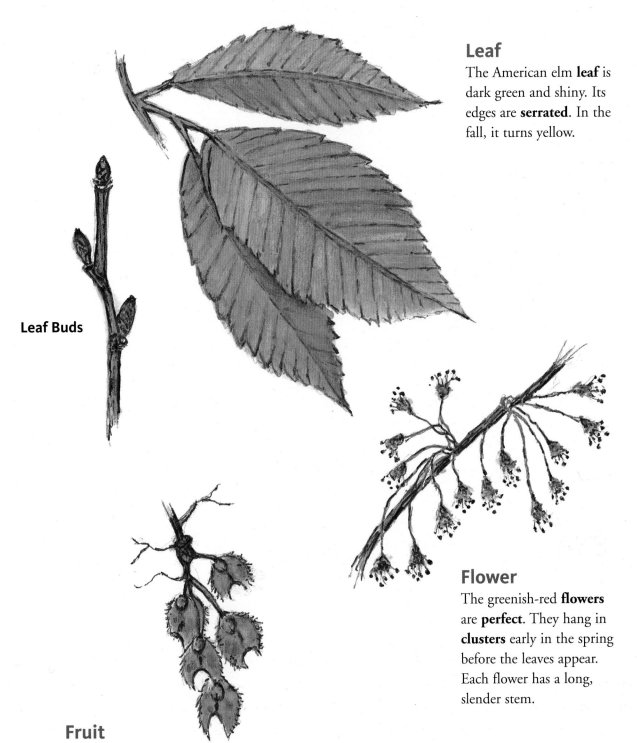

Leaf

The American elm **leaf** is dark green and shiny. Its edges are **serrated**. In the fall, it turns yellow.

Leaf Buds

Flower

The greenish-red **flowers** are **perfect**. They hang in **clusters** early in the spring before the leaves appear. Each flower has a long, slender stem.

Fruit

The greenish, flat **fruit** are **samaras**. Papery-thin wings surround a flat **seed**. They are rounded and notched and fringed with "hairs." The fruit usually ripen as the new leaves unfold in the spring.

EMPRESS TREE
Paulownia tomentosa
(paw-**low**-nee-uh toe-men-**toe**-sah)

Also called
royal paulownia

Native to China

Deciduous
40 feet tall and
40 feet wide

Spring

The paulownia or empress tree was named for Anna Paulownia. She was the granddaughter of Catherine the Great, a ruler of Russia in the 1700s. The empress tree grows very fast—it can grow ten feet or more in one just season. New trees often sprout from old empress tree **stumps**. Trees that grow this fast sometimes crowd out other, more slow-growing trees. Plants that crowd out delicate native plants are called **invasive** because they can invade a natural area and take it over. In cities, empress trees usually grow in places where other plants could not survive.

For centuries, people in China have made medicines from this tree's wood, **flowers**, and **fruit**. Japanese people used the wood to make rice pots, bowls, spoons, crates, sandals, and furniture. They also made stringed instruments called lutes from empress wood. It's thought that empress tree seeds first arrived in the United States when the **pods** were packed as protection around delicate products sent from China.

Leaf Bud

Leaf

The **leaf** is medium to dark green and "hairy" underneath. In fall, leaves usually drop off when they are still green. Leaves on young trees are huge—some can be used like umbrellas. Leaves on older trees are might smaller but still be a foot long.

Fruit

Ripe **fruit capsules** split at the end into two parts. Each capsule contains up to 2,000 small **winged seeds**. A large tree may produce 20 million seeds a year!

Flower

The bell-shaped **flowers** are pale violet with darker spots and yellow stripes. In the spring, they hang in long **clusters** called **panicles**. They smell like vanilla! Brown **flower buds** form in the fall and are often killed in cold winter weather.

WHITE FIR
Abies concolor
(**ay**-beez **kon**-kul-er)

Native to western
and southwestern U.S.

Evergreen
50–100 feet tall

Winter

The white fir gets its name from its light-colored **bark** and bluish or grayish-green **needles**. The needles are long—almost like a pine's. You can easily identify white fir by looking at its needles and **cones**. The needles are flat. The base of the needle is wide, sort of like a suction cup. When it's pulled away from the **twig**, it leaves a round, dented **leaf scar**. When the needles are crushed, they smell like tangerine or lemon.

Fir cones don't hang downward but rather stand upright on top of the branch. You can't save fir cones for holiday decorations because they don't last: When the cone opens to release the seeds, the **scales** shatter (break apart), and all that's left is a bare stalk.

Some people use white fir **pitch** (the sticky substance that oozes from the bark) to treat wounds. Tan-colored dye is made from the bark. Because the wood has no smell of its own, it makes good tubs for storing foods. The white fir is also hardy. It tolerates hot weather and can live with little water longer than most firs.

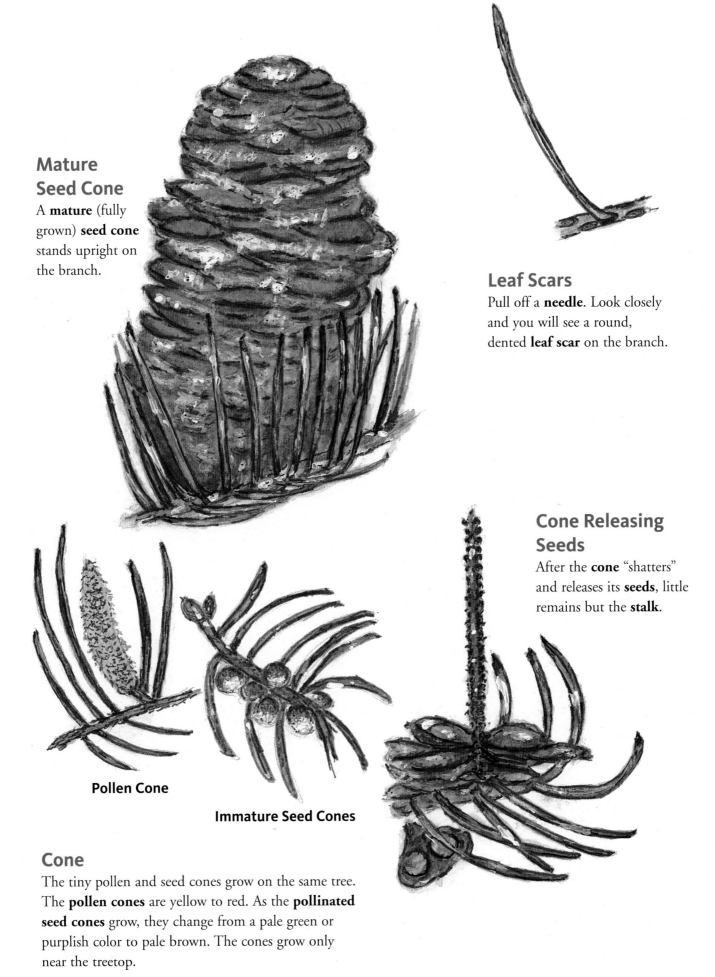

Mature Seed Cone

A **mature** (fully grown) **seed cone** stands upright on the branch.

Leaf Scars

Pull off a **needle**. Look closely and you will see a round, dented **leaf scar** on the branch.

Cone Releasing Seeds

After the **cone** "shatters" and releases its **seeds**, little remains but the **stalk**.

Pollen Cone

Immature Seed Cones

Cone

The tiny pollen and seed cones grow on the same tree. The **pollen cones** are yellow to red. As the **pollinated seed cones** grow, they change from a pale green or purplish color to pale brown. The cones grow only near the treetop.

FRANKLINIA
Franklinia alatamaha
(frank-**lin**-ee-ah ah-**lah**-tah-**mah**-hah)

Originally native to Georgia, eastern U.S.

Extinct in the wild

Deciduous
10–20 feet tall

Summer

The franklinia is a small tree with an interesting history. Around 1765, a plant scientist or **botanist** named John Bartram and his son, William, were exploring along the Alatamaha (now called Altamaha) River in Georgia. They saw a lovely small tree with cup-shaped white **flowers**. They were heading for Florida and didn't have time to stop and collect its **seeds**. But a few years later, William went back for some and planted them back home in Philadelphia.

John Bartram had never seen a tree like it, and he named it after his friend Benjamin Franklin, a very important man when America was a young country. He was an inventor, writer, and the U.S. ambassador to France.

Strangely enough, after 1803, when people went to Georgia to collect more franklinias, none were found. The tree is **extinct** in the wild. It seems that all the franklinia trees alive today are descended from the seeds that grew in John Bartram's garden!

Leaf
The franklinia's **simple leaf** is shiny, dark green and wider in the middle than at the ends. It turns bright red or orange in the fall.

Leaf Bud

Seeds

Fruit
The **fruit** is an unusual woody **capsule** that contains several flat **seeds**. When it's ripe, it splits into five parts to release the seeds.

Flower
The **flower** is **perfect** and slightly cup-shaped. It has five white **petals** and a center of bright yellow **stamens**. This fragrant flower blooms in late July or early August. Sometimes it blooms as late as September.

THE GIANTS

Two kinds of enormous **conifers**, the giant sequoia and the California redwood, grow on the west coast of the United States. They live to be very, very old. Their thick **bark** helps to protect them from fire, insects, and disease. Most of these trees were cut down because people wanted to use their beautiful wood. But now people are trying to keep them safe in national and state parks. Both trees are named the official state tree of California.

GIANT SEQUOIA
Sequoiadendron giganteum
(suh-**kwoi**-uh-**den**-druhn jy-**gan**-tee-um)

Also called big tree

Native to the west slopes of the Sierra Nevada mountains in eastern California

State tree of California

CALIFORNIA REDWOOD
Sequoia sempervirens
(suh-**kwoi**-uh sem-per-**vye**-renz)

Also called coast redwood

Native to the Pacific coast from southern Oregon down to Monterey, California

State tree of California

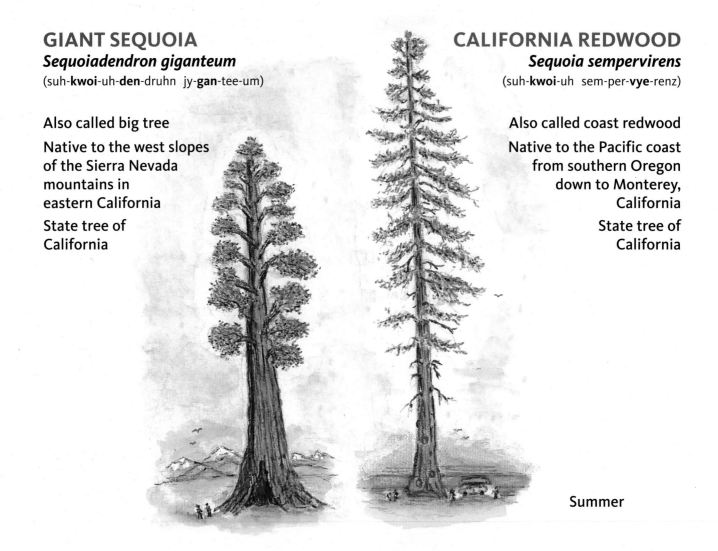

Summer

Giant sequoia trees have the largest **trunks** in the world. Their bark is almost three feet thick, and the trunk can grow 40 feet across. That's as wide as some houses! The oldest giant sequoias have been alive for about 3,000 years.

California redwoods are the world's tallest conifers. They can reach heights of 393 feet. That's about as tall as a 40-story building! Some of these trees are at least 1,000 years old.

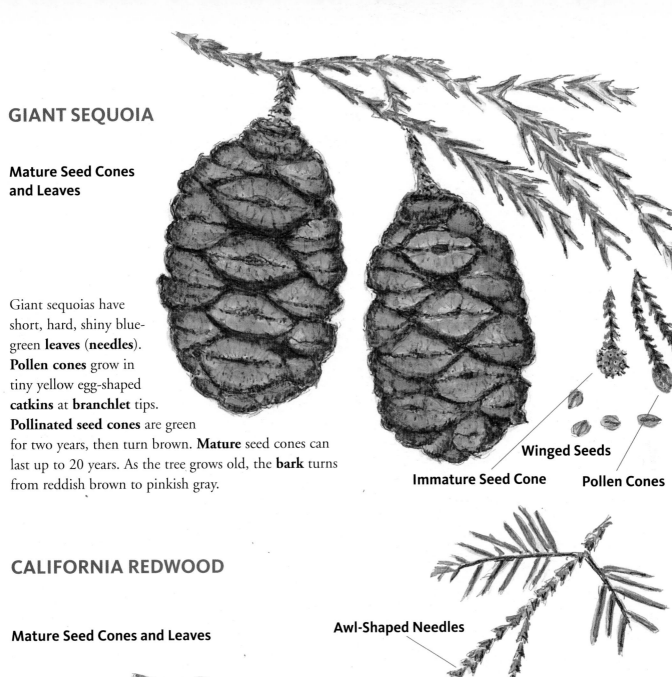

GIANT SEQUOIA

**Mature Seed Cones
and Leaves**

Giant sequoias have
short, hard, shiny blue-
green **leaves** (**needles**).
Pollen cones grow in
tiny yellow egg-shaped
catkins at **branchlet** tips.
Pollinated seed cones are green
for two years, then turn brown. **Mature** seed cones can
last up to 20 years. As the tree grows old, the **bark** turns
from reddish brown to pinkish gray.

Winged Seeds

Immature Seed Cone

Pollen Cones

CALIFORNIA REDWOOD

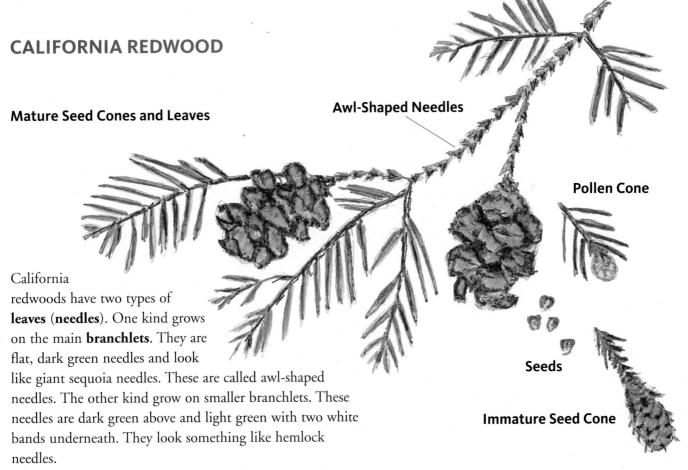

Mature Seed Cones and Leaves

Awl-Shaped Needles

Pollen Cone

California
redwoods have two types of
leaves (**needles**). One kind grows
on the main **branchlets**. They are
flat, dark green needles and look
like giant sequoia needles. These are called awl-shaped
needles. The other kind grow on smaller branchlets. These
needles are dark green above and light green with two white
bands underneath. They look something like hemlock
needles.

Seeds

Immature Seed Cone

GINKGO
Ginkgo biloba
(**gink**-o by-**low**-ba)

**Also called
maidenhair tree**
Originally native to China
Extinct in the wild

**Deciduous
50–80 feet tall
Dates back to
prehistoric times**

Fall

It's believed that ginkgos have been growing on earth for 150 million years. Sometimes a plant leaves its imprint in mud or clay. If the mud is buried for a very long time, it can become rock. The imprints left in rock by plants and animals from long ago are called **fossils**. Three-million-year-old ginkgo **leaf** fossils have been found in China, and today, ginkgo trees are nicknamed "living fossils."

Ginkgos are sacred trees in Korea, Japan, and China. Thousands of years ago, Chinese Buddhist priests took ginkgos from forests and planted them in temple gardens. Eventually, ginkgos disappeared in the wild. The priests probably saved the ginkgo from becoming **extinct**.

A plant called the maidenhair fern has fan-shaped leaves something like a ginkgo's. That's why the ginkgo is also called the maidenhair tree. Because of the tree's leaf shape, people in China call it the duck's foot tree. Ginkgo **seeds** are smelly! But the inner part of the seed is a popular food in Asia.

It may take 20 to 50 years before a ginkgo tree is old enough to bear **flowers** and seeds. Ginkgos are good city street trees. They can withstand pollution, heat, cold, wind, and insects. Their corky-looking wood is supposed to be resistant to fire.

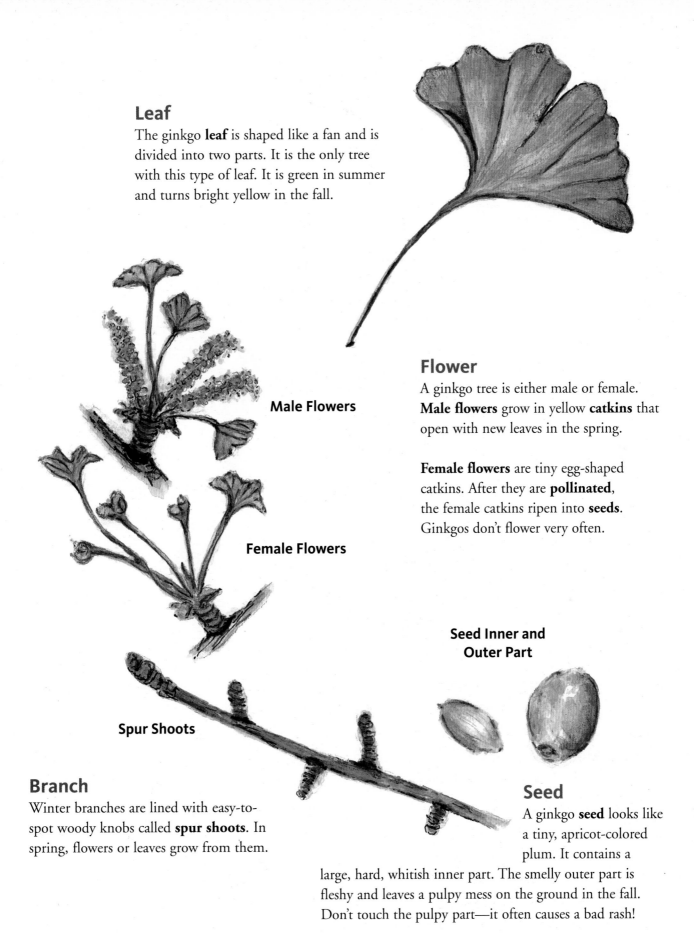

Leaf

The ginkgo **leaf** is shaped like a fan and is divided into two parts. It is the only tree with this type of leaf. It is green in summer and turns bright yellow in the fall.

Male Flowers

Female Flowers

Flower

A ginkgo tree is either male or female. **Male flowers** grow in yellow **catkins** that open with new leaves in the spring.

Female flowers are tiny egg-shaped catkins. After they are **pollinated**, the female catkins ripen into **seeds**. Ginkgos don't flower very often.

Seed Inner and Outer Part

Spur Shoots

Branch

Winter branches are lined with easy-to-spot woody knobs called **spur shoots**. In spring, flowers or leaves grow from them.

Seed

A ginkgo **seed** looks like a tiny, apricot-colored plum. It contains a large, hard, whitish inner part. The smelly outer part is fleshy and leaves a pulpy mess on the ground in the fall. Don't touch the pulpy part—it often causes a bad rash!

GOLDEN-RAIN TREE
Koelreuteria paniculata
(kol-roo-**teh**-ree-ah   pan-**ick**-u-**lah**-tah)

Also called
varnish tree, pride of India,
China tree
Native to China,
Korea, and Japan

Deciduous
30–40 feet tall

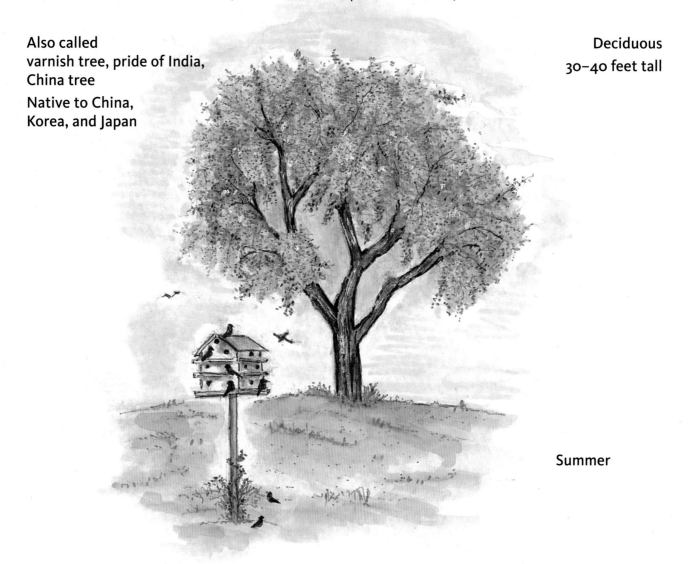

Summer

The golden-rain tree once grew only in Asia, where it was a favorite tree. In China, when an important government official died, a golden-rain tree was often planted next to the grave. A French Jesuit priest living in China sent some **seeds** in a camel caravan to Europe around 1750. Soon after, the golden-rain tree seeds were planted in public gardens in England and France.

Thomas Jefferson, the third president of the United States, was very interested in plants. Around 1809, his good friend Countess de Tesse sent him some golden-rain tree seeds from France. President Jefferson grew them in his garden in Monticello, his home in Virginia. It's said that they were the first golden-rain trees planted in North America. Today, golden-rain trees still live at Monticello.

The golden-rain tree is one of the few trees with yellow **flowers** that can grow in cool climates. The flowers appear in July. Most trees bloom earlier in the year. The **fruit** is unusual. It looks like a puffy, three-sided, papery heart.

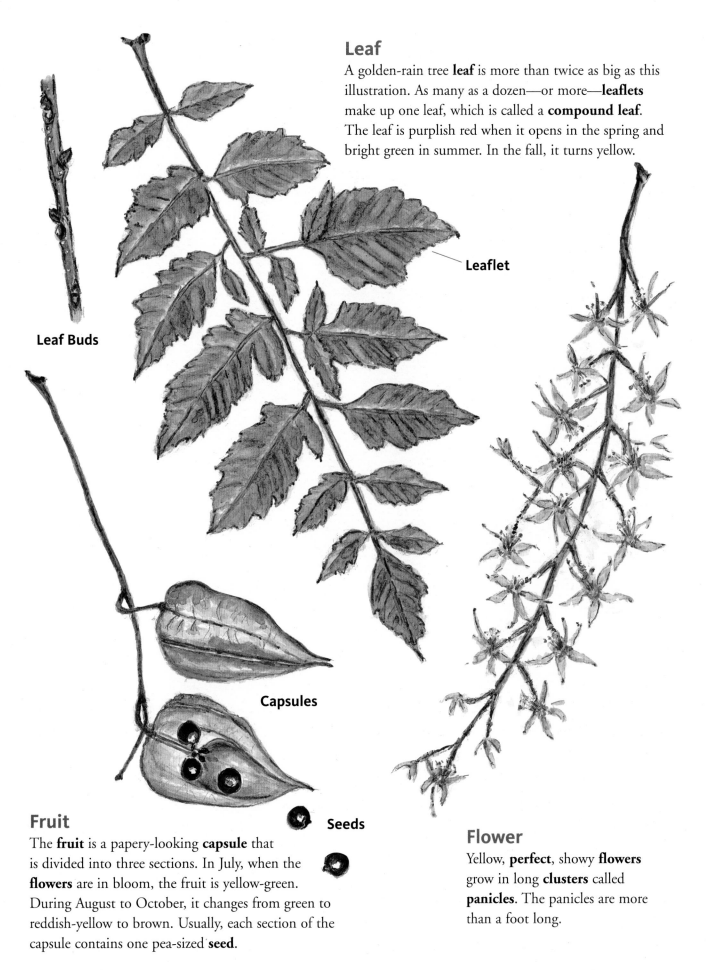

Leaf

A golden-rain tree **leaf** is more than twice as big as this illustration. As many as a dozen—or more—**leaflets** make up one leaf, which is called a **compound leaf**. The leaf is purplish red when it opens in the spring and bright green in summer. In the fall, it turns yellow.

Leaflet

Leaf Buds

Capsules

Fruit

The **fruit** is a papery-looking **capsule** that is divided into three sections. In July, when the **flowers** are in bloom, the fruit is yellow-green. During August to October, it changes from green to reddish-yellow to brown. Usually, each section of the capsule contains one pea-sized **seed**.

Seeds

Flower

Yellow, **perfect**, showy **flowers** grow in long **clusters** called **panicles**. The panicles are more than a foot long.

EASTERN HEMLOCK
Tsuga canadensis
(**tsoo**-gah **ca**-nah-**den**-sis)

Also called
Canadian hemlock
Native to North America

Evergreen
40–70 feet tall;
can grow to 100 feet tall
State tree of
Pennsylvania

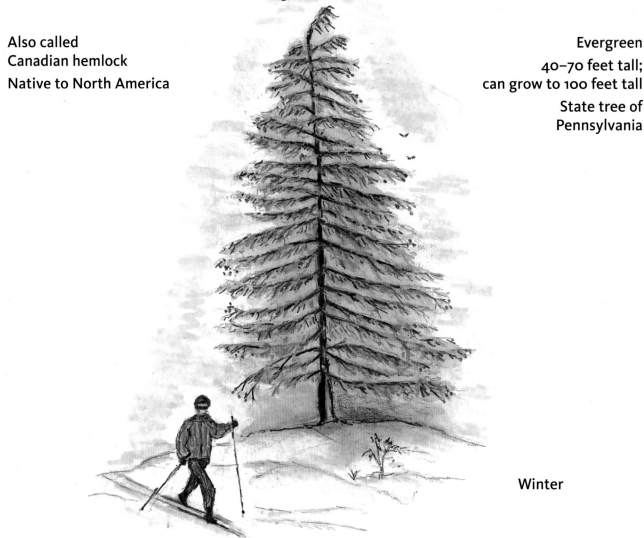

Winter

The eastern hemlock is a graceful tree with drooping branches that sometimes touch the ground. You can easily identify a hemlock by looking at its **habit**, **needles**, and **cones**. The tree's very top **branchlet** usually droops to one side like a little flag. The hemlock's tiny cones grow only at the ends of the branchlets.

Early settlers and American Indians made tea from the **twigs** and needles. They made red dye from the **bark** and swept with brooms of hemlock branchlets. The Indians also boiled the bark and pounded it into a paste that they put on wounds to help them heal. There is a strong poison called hemlock. It doesn't come from this tree but from a smaller plant with the same name.

The eastern hemlock can't take wind or very dry or wet soil. It's one of the few evergreens that can grow in shade. Eastern hemlock wood is hard and brittle. It doesn't last a long time, but it has very tough areas called **knots** in it. If you burn hemlock wood, be careful. It shoots out sparks!

Leaf

Eastern hemlock **needles** are tiny and flat. They are shiny dark green on top with two silvery bands underneath. When you pull off a hemlock needle, a woody base is left on the **branchlet**.

The Life of a Hemlock

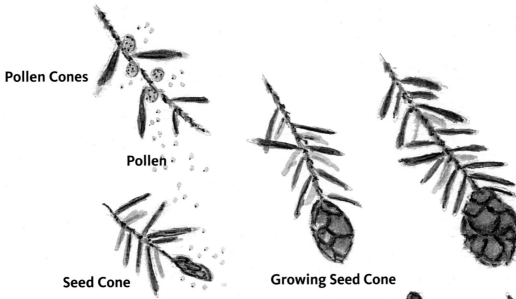

Pollen Cones

Pollen

Seed Cone

Growing Seed Cone

Ripe Seed Cone with Opening Scales

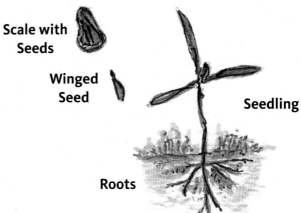

Scale with Seeds

Winged Seed

Seedling

Roots

Cone and Seedling

The eastern hemlock has tiny **pollen cones** and **seed cones**. After the seed cones are **pollinated**, they grow into full-sized cones. When the ripe cone opens its **scales**, its **winged seeds** land on the ground and sprout. **Roots** are sent into the soil and a **seedling** starts to grow into a new hemlock tree.

SHAGBARK HICKORY
Carya ovata
(**car**-ee-ah o-**vay**-tah)

Native to eastern U.S.

Deciduous
60–80 feet tall

Fall

The shagbark hickory belongs to the walnut family. *Hickory* is an Algonquin American Indian word for a milky food obtained from the **nuts** of this tree. To make it, people soaked nut kernels (the part you eat) in boiling water. Then they pounded the kernels and saved the liquid from them. They used the sweet, oily milk when they made corn cakes. The American Indians also took doses of hickory nut oil to treat stomachaches.

The tree is also named for its shaggy **bark**. The bark is smooth on young trees, but on old trees it breaks away at the top and bottom. Then it curls off in shaggy strips. Early American colonists made a yellow dye from the inner bark.

Chips of hickory wood are often used to barbecue meat. Meats cooked over hickory wood fires have a smoky flavor. Hickory wood is tough and heavy. It's made into strong baseball bats. American axes are popular all over the world because of their sturdy hickory handles.

Andrew Jackson, the seventh president of the United States, was nicknamed "Old Hickory" because he was so tough!

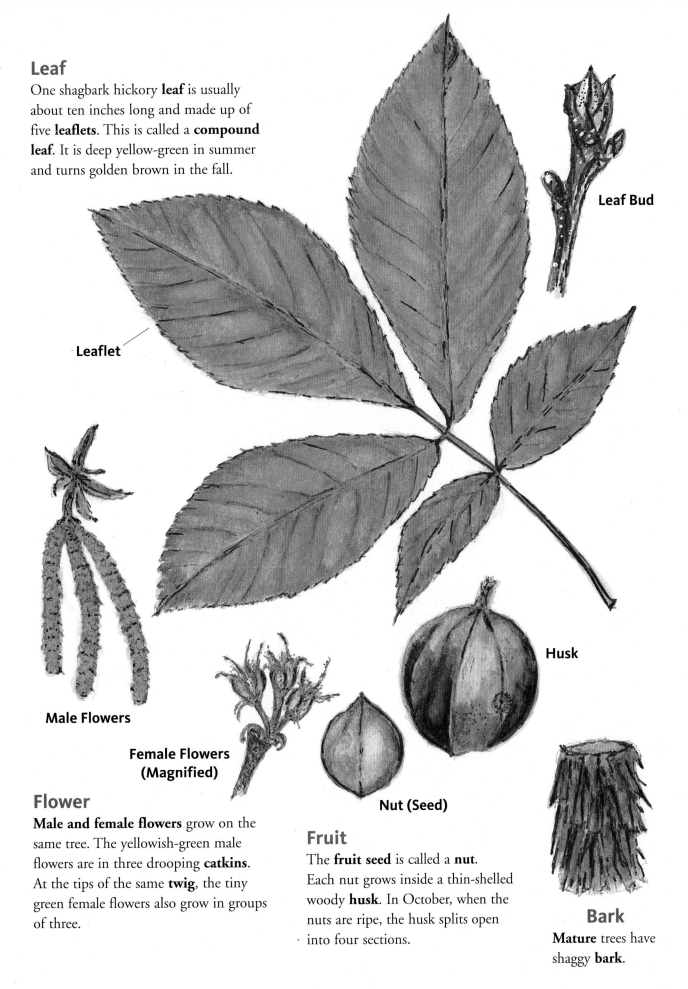

Leaf

One shagbark hickory **leaf** is usually about ten inches long and made up of five **leaflets**. This is called a **compound leaf**. It is deep yellow-green in summer and turns golden brown in the fall.

Leaflet

Leaf Bud

Male Flowers

Female Flowers (Magnified)

Flower

Male and female flowers grow on the same tree. The yellowish-green male flowers are in three drooping **catkins**. At the tips of the same **twig**, the tiny green female flowers also grow in groups of three.

Husk

Nut (Seed)

Fruit

The **fruit seed** is called a **nut**. Each nut grows inside a thin-shelled woody **husk**. In October, when the nuts are ripe, the husk splits open into four sections.

Bark

Mature trees have shaggy **bark**.

HONEY LOCUST
Gleditsia triacanthos
(gle-**ditz**-see-ah try-a-**can**-thos)

Native to
North America

Deciduous
50–80 feet tall

Fall

The honey locust is a popular street tree because it needs little care. Its **leaves** are narrow and fine. When they fall to the ground, they usually shrivel and blow away. For many people, this is a good thing—the leaves don't need to be raked up!

In late spring, bees sip **nectar** from the tree's tiny **flowers**. In summer, the long, curly **fruit pods** grow. When they first appear the pods are yellow-green. By late autumn the pods turn dark reddish brown, fall to the ground, and are eagerly eaten by cattle and wild animals. The **seeds** inside are covered by a gummy pulp that tastes sweet, which is why the tree is called honey locust.

Honey locust wood is hard and heavy. Because it doesn't rot easily when it's standing in soil, this wood is perfect for fence posts, poles, and railroad ties. The **bark** has bunches of sharp three-pointed **thorns** growing from it. They can be four inches long.

There is a honey locust **variety** called *inermis* that has no pods or thorns.

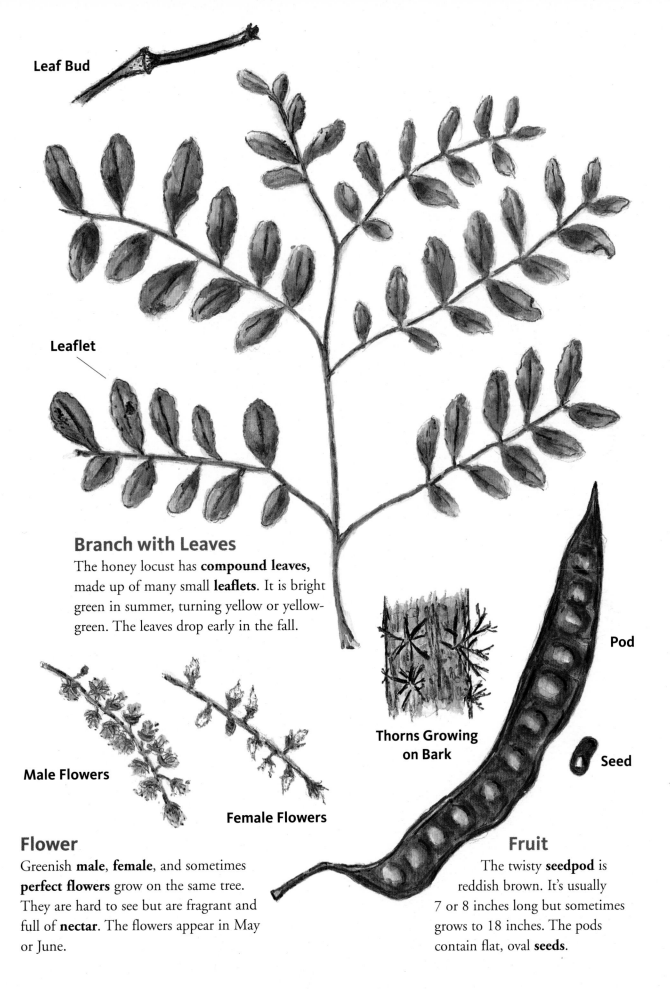

Leaf Bud

Leaflet

Branch with Leaves

The honey locust has **compound leaves,** made up of many small **leaflets**. It is bright green in summer, turning yellow or yellow-green. The leaves drop early in the fall.

Male Flowers

Female Flowers

Thorns Growing on Bark

Pod

Seed

Flower

Greenish **male**, **female**, and sometimes **perfect flowers** grow on the same tree. They are hard to see but are fragrant and full of **nectar**. The flowers appear in May or June.

Fruit

The twisty **seedpod** is reddish brown. It's usually 7 or 8 inches long but sometimes grows to 18 inches. The pods contain flat, oval **seeds**.

HORSE CHESTNUT
Aesculus hippocastanum
(es-**koo**-lus hip-o-kas-**tay**-num)

Native to Balkan
peninsula and
mountains of
Greece and Albania

Deciduous
50–75 feet tall

Spring

The horse chestnut has a **habit** that makes this tree easy to identify. The wide, spreading branches swoop toward the ground, flipping up at the ends. Hundreds of **flowers** bloom on this tree in the spring, attracting bees to the **nectar**.

Horse chestnut **bark** has been used in medicines, and in Turkey, people once used a medicine from the **nuts** to treat sick horses. That's how the tree got its name. However, it's thought that it sometimes made the horses sicker. Don't ever confuse horse chestnut nuts with the chestnuts you buy to eat! Fresh horse chestnut nuts are bitter and poisonous. When they are ground up they make a good library paste. Some people believe they won't get arthritis if they carry the nuts in their pockets.

Horse chestnut wood is easy to carve. It is often used by toy makers and woodcarvers. The horse chestnut is a popular European street tree. They are handsome trees, but if you look closely from early summer on, you'll see that the **leaves** have gotten a leaf blotch disease. It makes them brown and shriveled along the edges.

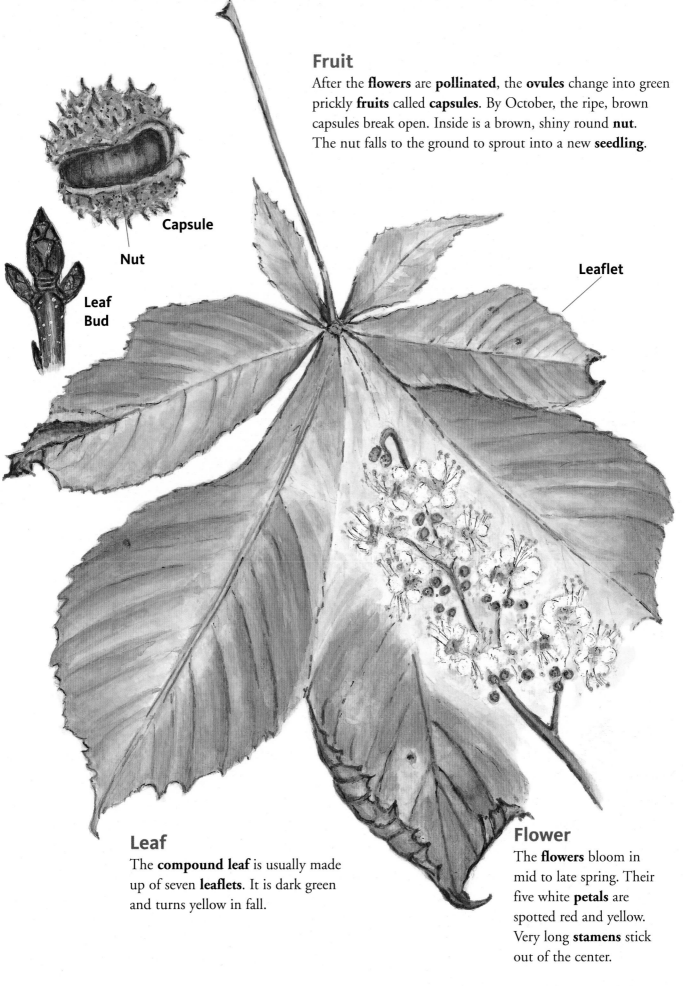

Fruit

After the **flowers** are **pollinated**, the **ovules** change into green prickly **fruits** called **capsules**. By October, the ripe, brown capsules break open. Inside is a brown, shiny round **nut**. The nut falls to the ground to sprout into a new **seedling**.

Capsule

Nut

Leaf Bud

Leaflet

Leaf

The **compound leaf** is usually made up of seven **leaflets**. It is dark green and turns yellow in fall.

Flower

The **flowers** bloom in mid to late spring. Their five white **petals** are spotted red and yellow. Very long **stamens** stick out of the center.

AMERICAN LARCH
Larix laricina
(**lar**-ix lar-eh-**see**-nah)

Also called
tamarack, eastern larch

Native to Canada and
northern U.S.

Deciduous conifer
40–80 feet tall

Summer

The American larch is often called the tamarack. This comes from the Algonquian American Indian word *hackmatack*. It is a **conifer** with **leaves** that look like needles. But it isn't an **evergreen** tree. It is **deciduous**. In the fall, all the **needles** turn yellow and drop off. In the spring, new needles grow back and the tree again looks like an evergreen.

The American larch can grow in very cold climates. It can live in wet or damp soil. The tree's **cones** look like little wooden roses. When the tree is between 50 and 150 years old, it might have 20,000 cones a year. This means that one American larch could make 300,000 **seeds** in one year!

American larch wood is strong and heavy. It is used for telephone poles, fence posts, and shipbuilding. American Indians found the larch a very useful tree. Using the **roots** as heavy thread, they stitched strips of birch bark onto their canoes. They used the wood for arrow shafts and made medicine from the **bark**.

Each year, porcupines kill or damage many American larches. These animals like to eat the inner bark. To get at it, they strip off the outer bark. Without its outer bark, a tree will die.

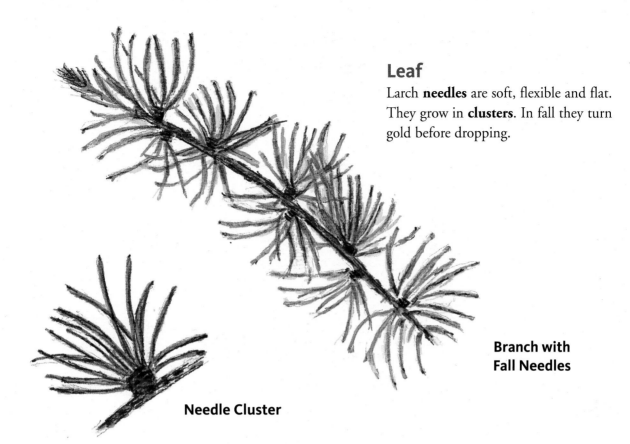

Leaf

Larch **needles** are soft, flexible and flat. They grow in **clusters**. In fall they turn gold before dropping.

**Branch with
Fall Needles**

Needle Cluster

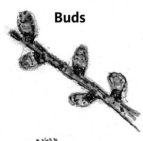

Buds

Winter Branch

During the winter the larch branches are bare. Only the **buds** are left behind, waiting for spring.

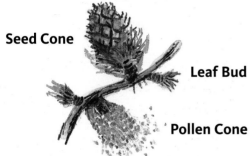

Seed Cone

Leaf Bud

Pollen Cone

Cone

In the spring, the **buds** grow into **needles**, **cones**, and **flowers**. The **pollen cones pollinate** the **seed cones**.

As the **seed cone** grows, it starts to look like a tiny brown wooden rose. When the cone is ripe, the **scales** open and the **seeds** "fly away" on tiny wings. When they land on the ground, they sprout, and a new larch begins to grow.

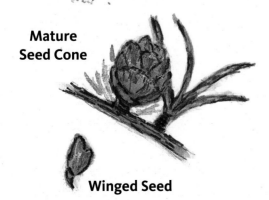

**Mature
Seed Cone**

Winged Seed

SAUCER MAGNOLIA
Magnolia x soulangiana
(mag-**no**-lee-ah ex soo-**lan**-gee-**aye**-nuh)

A hybrid first grown in
France in 1820

Not found in the wild

Semievergreen
20–30 feet tall

Spring

The saucer magnolia is a **hybrid** tree. The "×" in its name means that it is a cross (combination) of two different **species** or kinds of magnolias.

In France, around 1820, a Frenchman named Etienne Soulange-Bodin grew the first saucer magnolia. He was a retired soldier who had fought in Napoleon's army. Monsieur Soulange-Bodin was also a plant grower. Two kinds of magnolias grew in his garden. They came from China. One kind had very large white **flowers**. The other kind had smaller purple flowers. When the **pollen** and **seeds** of these two magnolias were combined, a new kind of magnolia grew. It had large pink flowers. It was named the saucer magnolia.

Saucer magnolias are grown for their beautiful flowers. The flowers bloom when the tree is still very young and no taller than two or three feet. In warm climates, the **leaves** stay on the tree all year. In cooler climates, the leaves drop off in autumn. The flowers appear before new leaves grow in the spring. Unfortunately, if there is a late frost, the **flower buds** may freeze. Then, that year, there are no flowers.

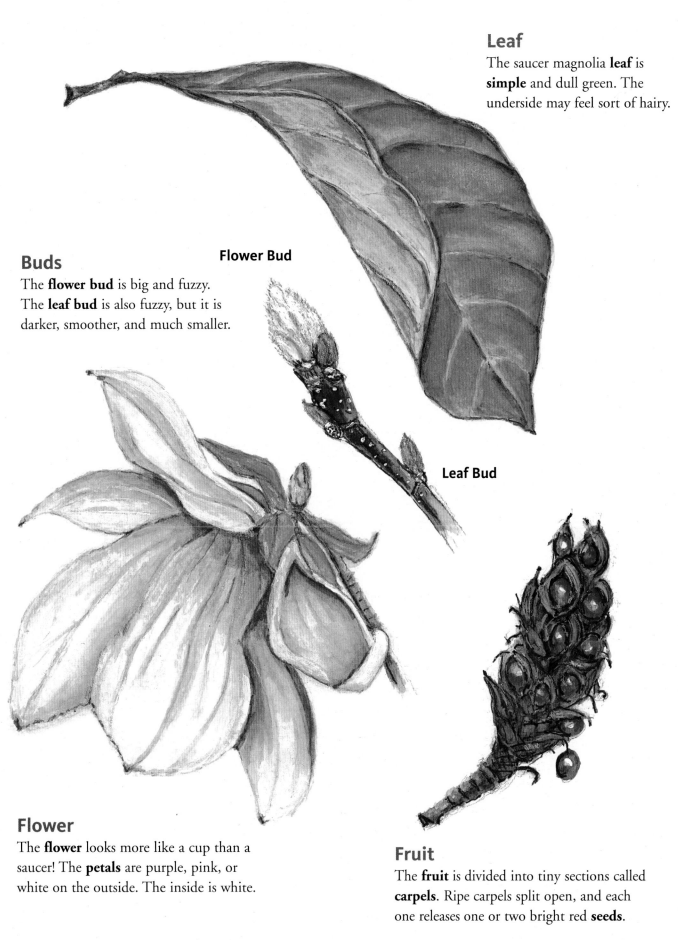

Leaf

The saucer magnolia **leaf** is **simple** and dull green. The underside may feel sort of hairy.

Flower Bud

Buds

The **flower bud** is big and fuzzy. The **leaf bud** is also fuzzy, but it is darker, smoother, and much smaller.

Leaf Bud

Flower

The **flower** looks more like a cup than a saucer! The **petals** are purple, pink, or white on the outside. The inside is white.

Fruit

The **fruit** is divided into tiny sections called **carpels**. Ripe carpels split open, and each one releases one or two bright red **seeds**.

SUGAR MAPLE
Acer saccharum
(**ay**-sir **sak**-kar-um)

Also called
rock maple, hard maple

Native to eastern
North America

Deciduous

60–100 feet

State tree of
New York, Vermont,
West Virginia,
and Wisconsin

Fall

The sugar maple has very important **sap**. For hundreds of years, American Indians seasoned their meat with the sticky liquid. Later, they taught the pioneers how to collect the sap by "tapping" the trees—boring a hole in the **trunk**, pushing a spout into the hole, and collecting sap in a hanging bucket. The sap is boiled and made into maple syrup and maple sugar candy. It takes about 40 gallons of sap to make 1 gallon of syrup or 8 pounds of sugar. After the watery sap dries on the tree, it leaves behind a sugary crust that the squirrels like to eat.

Sugar maple wood is so hard and heavy it's called "rock" or "hard" maple. It is used for making tools, cabinets, furniture, floors, and bowling alleys. Sometimes the wood has unusual patterns in it. If the **annual rings** are wavy, the wood is called curly or fiddleback maple. Wood with a dotted pattern is bird's-eye maple. These patterned maple woods are special and expensive. Every fall, people from all over the world travel to New England to see the brilliantly colored sugar maple leaves.

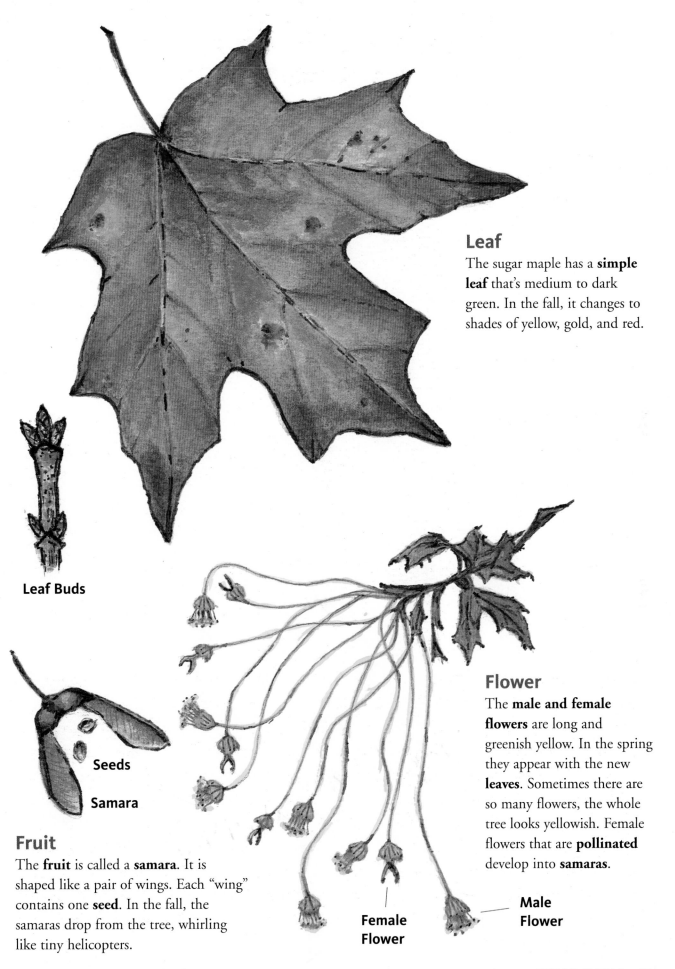

Leaf

The sugar maple has a **simple leaf** that's medium to dark green. In the fall, it changes to shades of yellow, gold, and red.

Leaf Buds

Seeds

Samara

Fruit

The **fruit** is called a **samara**. It is shaped like a pair of wings. Each "wing" contains one **seed**. In the fall, the samaras drop from the tree, whirling like tiny helicopters.

Flower

The **male and female flowers** are long and greenish yellow. In the spring they appear with the new **leaves**. Sometimes there are so many flowers, the whole tree looks yellowish. Female flowers that are **pollinated** develop into **samaras**.

Female Flower

Male Flower

MIMOSA TREE
Albizia julibrissin
(a-**biz**-ee-uh ju-lee-**bris**-in)

Also called
silk-tree

Native to Iran and
east to central China

Deciduous
30–45 feet tall

Summer

The mimosa tree is easy to spot. It's very different looking from other trees. The **leaves** are delicate and feathery. Strangest of all, they fold up at night. They stay green until they drop off in the fall.

The **flowers** are unusual and look like long, silky pink-and-white brushes. They bloom a long time, from mid-July to early September. Hummingbirds, bees, and butterflies find their sweet **nectar** a big attraction. In the fall, the mimosa tree has long **seedpods**. A plant with this type of fruit is called a **legume**. The honey locust on page 58 is also a legume.

The mimosa tree is native to China and important to the Chinese people. They prepare many kinds of medicines from the **bark**, leaves, and flowers. Its cooked flowers are also eaten like vegetables, and the dried leaves may be brewed into teas. An insect repellent is created from the bark. The wood is used in building and for making furniture.

Mimosa trees grow wild along roadsides and highways in the southern United States.

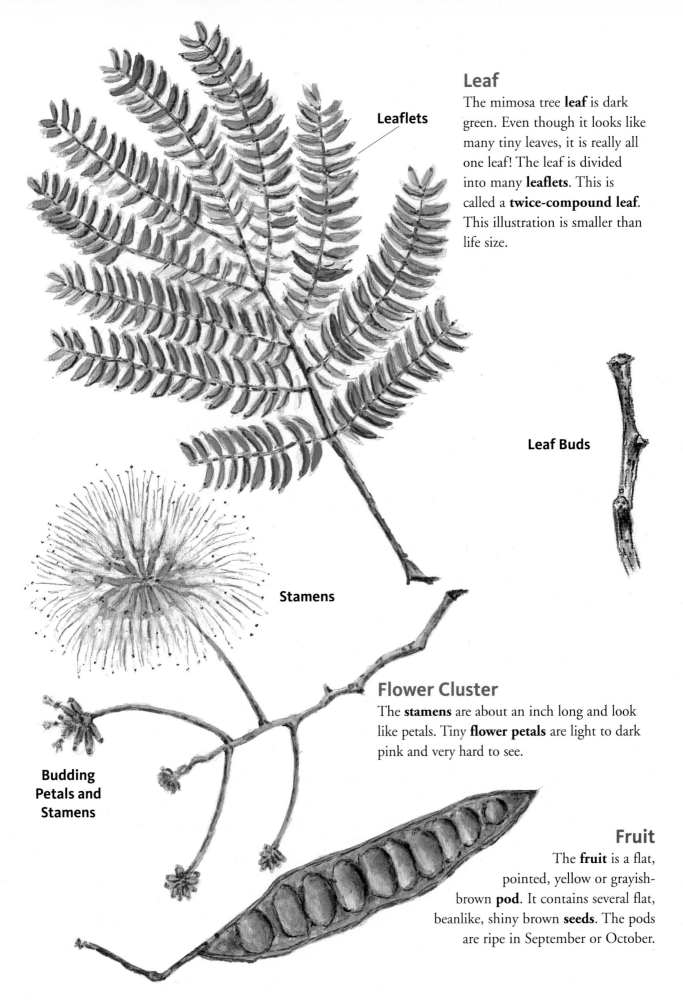

Leaflets

Leaf

The mimosa tree **leaf** is dark green. Even though it looks like many tiny leaves, it is really all one leaf! The leaf is divided into many **leaflets**. This is called a **twice-compound leaf**. This illustration is smaller than life size.

Leaf Buds

Stamens

Flower Cluster

The **stamens** are about an inch long and look like petals. Tiny **flower petals** are light to dark pink and very hard to see.

Budding Petals and Stamens

Fruit

The **fruit** is a flat, pointed, yellow or grayish-brown **pod**. It contains several flat, beanlike, shiny brown **seeds**. The pods are ripe in September or October.

WHITE OAK
Quercus alba
(**kwer**-kus **al**-bah)

Also called
stave oak

Native to eastern U.S.

Deciduous

80–100 feet tall

State tree of
Connecticut, Illinois,
and Maryland

Summer

The white oak is named for its light gray **bark**. Huge old white oaks often grow in the middle of unused farm fields. They grow very slowly and may live for hundreds of years.

The white oak's **fruit** is the **acorn**. If you boil it, it becomes sweet and can be eaten. Early settlers and American Indians boiled acorns or ground them into meal and flour for making bread. Acorns are an important food for some birds and wild animals.

White oak **seedlings** sprout from acorns that fall to the ground in autumn. But acorns often freeze before they can send **roots** down into the soil. Fortunately, squirrels bury acorns to be dug up later for winter food. Because they leave lots buried and uneaten, these little animals are responsible for many white oak seedlings that grow each year.

The white oak is one of the most valuable trees in the United States. The wood is heavy, hard, strong, and fine for furniture and floors. It's used for ladder rungs and railroad ties. The wood is waterproof, and early American shipbuilders constructed mighty sailing vessels with white oak. It is one of the best woods for making barrels. The wooden strips that form the barrel sides are called staves. That's why this tree is sometimes called the stave oak.

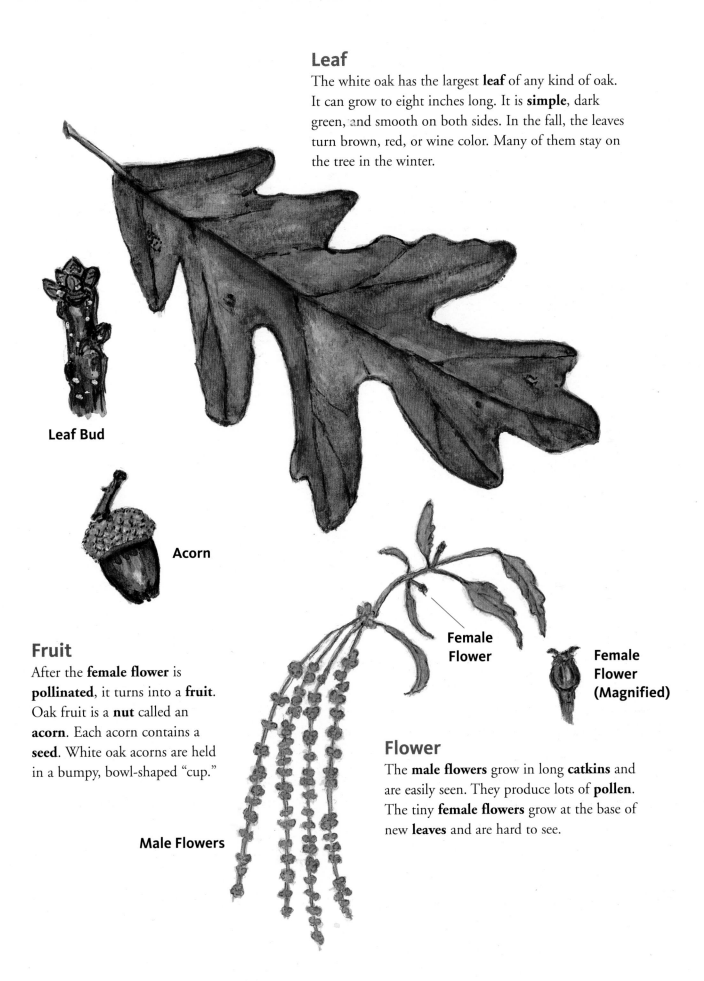

Leaf

The white oak has the largest **leaf** of any kind of oak. It can grow to eight inches long. It is **simple**, dark green, and smooth on both sides. In the fall, the leaves turn brown, red, or wine color. Many of them stay on the tree in the winter.

Leaf Bud

Acorn

Female Flower

Female Flower (Magnified)

Fruit

After the **female flower** is **pollinated**, it turns into a **fruit**. Oak fruit is a **nut** called an **acorn**. Each acorn contains a **seed**. White oak acorns are held in a bumpy, bowl-shaped "cup."

Male Flowers

Flower

The **male flowers** grow in long **catkins** and are easily seen. They produce lots of **pollen**. The tiny **female flowers** grow at the base of new **leaves** and are hard to see.

EASTERN WHITE PINE
Pinus strobus
(**pie**-nuss **strow**-bus)

Native to northeastern U.S.

Evergreen

Can grow more than 150 feet tall

State tree of Maine (the Pine State) and Michigan

Spring

The eastern white pine can grow in bare, dry places. It's the largest **conifer** in the northeastern United States and may live for hundreds of years.

The white pine has long been the symbol for peace for many American Indians. The tree's **needles**, growing in groups of five, stood for the Five Nations, which were tribes that had joined together. Later in American history, it was called the liberty tree. Its image was flown on the flags of early American colonies. The tulip tree, another tree in this book, is also called the liberty tree.

This tree changes with age. The young tree looks like a Christmas tree. Old eastern white pines have tall bare **trunks** with branches beginning high above the ground. The tall straight trunks were used for sailing-ship masts. The **bark** changes over time too. On young trees, it's thin and smooth. On very old trees, it's thick and deeply grooved. Rabbits and porcupines eat the bark of young trees. But it's the **seeds** that seem to be a favorite food of red squirrels and birds.

Leaf

Each **leaf** looks like a long green needle and is easy to bend. The **needles** grow in bundles called **fascicles**. The eastern white pine always has five needles in each fascicle.

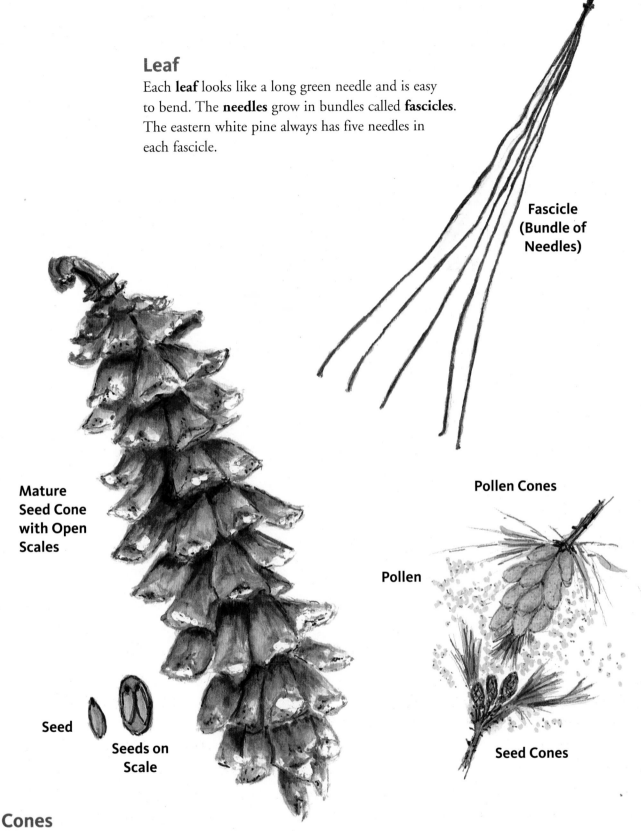

Fascicle (Bundle of Needles)

Mature Seed Cone with Open Scales

Pollen Cones

Pollen

Seed

Seeds on Scale

Seed Cones

Cones

Eastern white pines have **pollen cones** and **seed cones**. Both kinds grow on the same tree. The tiny yellow pollen cones grow in **clusters** and are covered with **pollen**. The seed cones are pink and made of soft **scales**. Each scale has two **ovules**. When the seed cone is pollinated by the pollen cone, the ovules turn into **seeds**. The scales become hard and close up to protect the seeds. The seed cone grows into a large yellow-brown cone. Then the cone dries out, the scales open, and the seeds blow away on tiny papery "wings."

LONDON PLANETREE
Platanus x acerifolia
(**plat**-ah-nus ex as-**er**-ih-**fo**-lee-uh)

Hybrid, first grown
in England in 1600s

Deciduous
70–100 feet tall

Summer

The London planetree is a **hybrid** (combination) of the sycamore tree of the eastern United States and the oriental planetree of southeastern Europe and Asia Minor. It was first noted around 1663 growing in London, England. It's believed that it was first grown by John Tradescant, the gardener to King Charles I of England. In 1635, he planted an American sycamore in his garden from seeds grown in Virginia. It is thought that seeds from this sycamore **cross-pollinated** with an oriental sycamore, and the first London planetree began to grow. They became very popular trees.

The London planetree is a good street tree. It grows in poor soil and can stand dry conditions and air pollution. On fully grown trees, the lowest branches are normally high up on the **trunk**, out of the way of traffic. The **fruits**, usually in pairs, hang in fuzzy balls made up of tiny **seeds**.

The **bark** is smooth and creamy yellow with patches of brown, green, and gray. It peels off in large flakes. Some people are allergic to the fuzz that comes off new **leaves** in the spring. The fuzzy young **twigs** in the summer may also bother people.

Leaf

The long wide **simple leaf** is green in the summer. In the fall, it turns yellow-brown.

Leaf Buds

Flower

The tiny **flowers** grow in ball-like **catkins** that hang from long green stalks. Male and female catkins grow on separate branches on the same tree. **Male catkins** are yellow-green. **Female catkins** are reddish green.

Female Catkins

Male Catkins

Fruit

The **fruit** are bristly brown balls that hang in pairs from a long stalk. They are made up of many hairy, tufted **nutlets** (**seeds**). Most balls stay on the tree all winter. When the balls break up in the fall or after the winter, they are very messy.

Fruit Ball

Tufted Nutlets

EASTERN REDCEDAR
Juniperus virginiana
(ju-**nip**-er-us vur-**jin**-ee-**ah**-nah)

**Also called
pencil cedar,
Virginian juniper**

Eastern U.S.

**Evergreen
40–50 feet tall**

Summer

The eastern redcedar is an **evergreen** that grows slowly and lives a long time. But it's not really a cedar. It is a type of tree called a juniper. It's often seen in old pastures and along the sides of roads. The trees usually stand close together in all sizes ranging from large trees to small, bushy ones. The wood lasts well outdoors, so early European colonists in Virginia built log cabins and made fence posts from eastern redcedar. To cut down the force of winds, farmers planted the trees across fields in lines called **windbreaks**.

The reddish-brown **bark** peels, by itself, in long strips. The pinkish-brown wood beneath is very fragrant. Because people like the way it smells, the eastern redcedar is a popular Christmas tree. And the odor keeps moths away! That's why the wood is used for moth-proof cedar chests and closets for storing clothes. It is also the world's best wood for making pencils. The pencils never split while they're being sharpened. Oil of cedar, made from the **leaves** and wood, is put into polishes, medicines, and perfumes. The eastern redcedar's ripe **seed cones** are food for many birds and other wild animals. They spread **seeds** over the land, and then more eastern redcedars appear.

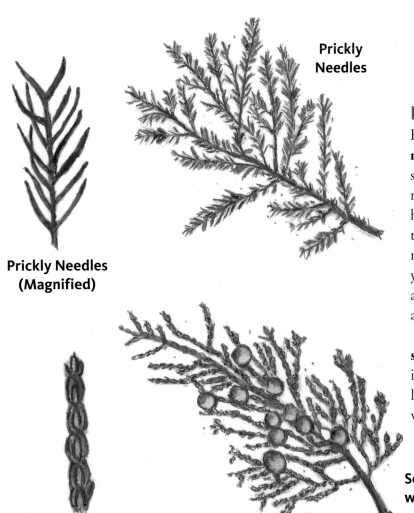

Prickly Needles

Prickly Needles (Magnified)

Scalelike Needles (Magnified)

Scalelike Needles with Pollinated Seed Cones

Leaf and Cone

Eastern redcedars have two kinds of **needles** (**leaves**). New needles are sharp and prickly. Older scalelike needles are smoother. The needles have a nice smell if you squeeze them between your fingers. Each needle stays on the tree five or six years and then it falls off. But there are so many other needles, the tree always stays green.

The tree has **cones**. When a **seed cone** is **pollinated**, it grows into a round blue cone that looks like a tiny berry. It's coated with a whitish waxy surface called **bloom**.

Cedar Gall and Spores

Apple cedar rust is a disease caused by a **fungus**. It needs two kinds of trees to keep it growing and spreading. A **cedar gall**, often called a **cedar apple**, grows on eastern redcedars. It looks a bit like a brown golf ball. In springtime wet weather, the gall sprouts long slimy "horns." They produce rust-colored **spores**, tiny as dust, that shoot into the air. Winds can carry spores three miles away. If spores land on apple trees, they damage the **leaves** and **fruit**. Infected leaves produce new spores. The wind blows them to redcedars in the area. These spores grow into cedar galls and the cycle continues.

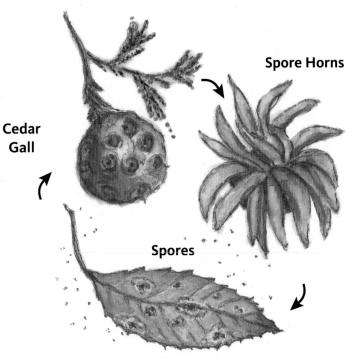

Cedar Gall

Spore Horns

Spores

Infected Apple Leaf

NORWAY SPRUCE
Picea abies
(**pie**-see-ah **ay**-bees)

Native to
north-central Europe

Evergreen
Usually 40–60 feet tall;
may grow to
100 feet tall or more

Winter

The Norway spruce needs lots of sunlight, but if it gets enough, it may grow as tall as a 10-story building. In the mountains in Germany, some Norway spruces are as much as 1,000 years old. As the tree grows older, the branches droop. This **habit** makes it easy to tell the Norway spruce from other **evergreens**. The **bark** also changes with age. It is reddish brown and very thin on young trees. By the time the tree is about 150 years old, the bark is thick with small gray, flaky scales. The Norway spruce has the largest **cones** of any kind of spruce.

American Indians cut the bark and chewed the **resin** that oozed from it. In the early 1800s, lumps of spruce resin were the first chewing gums sold in the United States.

Norway spruce wood is strong for its weight and is used in making paper. It also makes sturdy furniture and sounding boards for musical instruments. The **roots** can be twisted into strong rope. Spruce beer, a tasty soft drink, is made from the tree's new **leaves**. A Norway spruce doesn't make a good Christmas tree, because the **needles** fall off soon after it is brought indoors.

Leaf

A Norway spruce **leaf** looks like a short, stiff, green needle. The **needles** are bright green when they are young and become darker and shinier as they get older. They are four-sided and will roll between your fingers. Each needle stays on the tree several years before it falls off.

Leaf Scar

When you pull off a spruce **needle** from its branch, a short peg is left behind, which leaves the branch feeling prickly.

Winged Seed

Seed Cones

Pollen Cone

Cone

The Norway spruce grows pollen cones and seed cones on the same tree. The **pollen cones** are clusters of red **stamens** that turn yellow with **pollen** in early summer. The small **seed cones** are dark red or purplish and are pretty. After they are pollinated, the seed cones lose their bright color. They turn green and grow into a long cone that ripens in late summer or early fall. The cones usually fall from the tree when they are a year old.

Mature (Full-Grown) Seed Cone

SWEETGUM
Liquidambar styraciflua
(**lik**-wid-**am**-ber sty-**rass**-ih-**floo**-ah)

Also called
redgum, sapgum, alligator-tree, gumtree, bilsted
Native to eastern U.S.

Deciduous
65–75 feet tall

Winter

The sweetgum is named for its sweet-smelling **gum** (**sap**). The gum is collected by making cuts in the **bark** to allow the gum to ooze out. It is used in making perfume and some medicines. American pioneers peeled the bark and scraped off the solid coating of sap underneath. They chewed it like chewing gum. The **resin** was supposed to clean teeth and make breath smell sweet. Sweetgums are important timber trees. Because the wood gives a high polish (it can be rubbed to look shiny), it is used for making furniture and floors.

Sweetgums have beautiful autumn foliage. The star-shaped **leaves** turn many colors, often on the same tree. When the leaves begin to fall, they have a pleasant smell that often lasts until the leaves are shriveled and dry. It's easy to spot the golf-ball-size **fruit**. They fall from the tree by the hundreds. Each ball may hold more than 50 small **seeds**. They are eaten by squirrels, chipmunks, and birds. Lots of the prickly sweetgum balls hang on the tree all winter long.

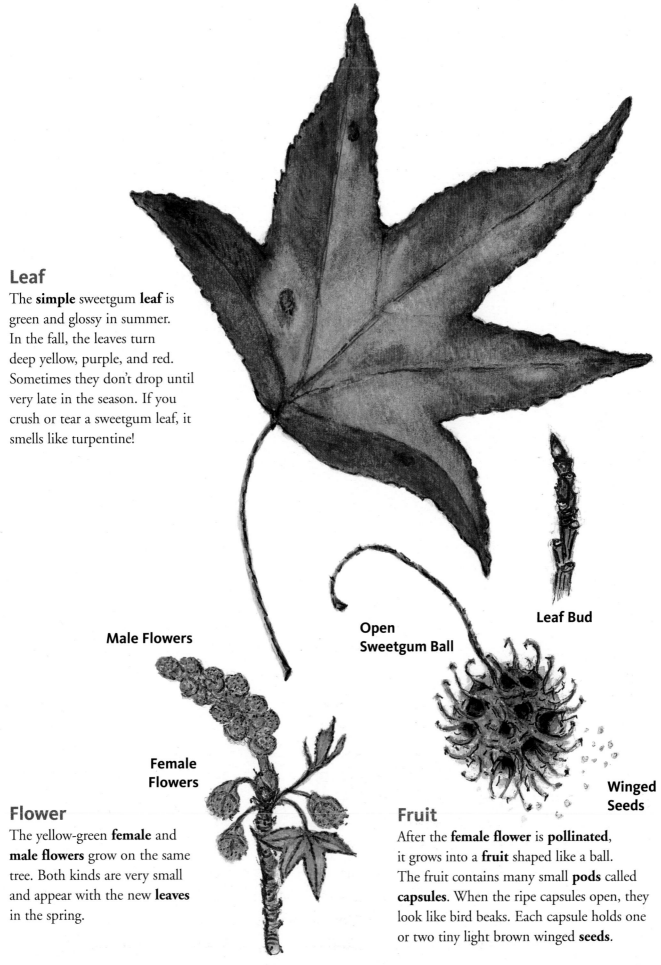

Leaf

The **simple** sweetgum **leaf** is green and glossy in summer. In the fall, the leaves turn deep yellow, purple, and red. Sometimes they don't drop until very late in the season. If you crush or tear a sweetgum leaf, it smells like turpentine!

Leaf Bud

Male Flowers

Open Sweetgum Ball

Female Flowers

Winged Seeds

Flower

The yellow-green **female** and **male flowers** grow on the same tree. Both kinds are very small and appear with the new **leaves** in the spring.

Fruit

After the **female flower** is **pollinated**, it grows into a **fruit** shaped like a ball. The fruit contains many small **pods** called **capsules**. When the ripe capsules open, they look like bird beaks. Each capsule holds one or two tiny light brown winged **seeds**.

TULIP TREE
Liriodendron tulipifera
(leer-ee-o-**den**-dron too-lih-**pif**-fur-ah)

Also called
yellow poplar, tulip poplar,
tulip magnolia, white wood
Native to eastern U.S.

Deciduous
Usually 70–90
feet tall; can
grow to more
than 180 feet tall
State tree of
Indiana and
Tennessee

Spring

The tulip tree is one of the tallest trees in the forest. It may live 200 years. The large, cup-shaped **flowers** don't appear until the tree is between 15 and 25 years old. They're hard to see because they grow high above the ground.

Tulip trees are weak-wooded. This means the limbs often break off during ice and wind storms. So it's not good to plant a tulip tree close to a building. Tulip tree wood is light yellow and easy to carve. American pioneers hollowed out logs to make long lightweight canoes. The wood is used nowadays for crates, musical instruments, toys, and roof shingles. The bitter-tasting **roots** and **bark** have been used in tonics and medicines and for making a golden-colored dye.

A historic tulip tree grew in Annapolis, Maryland. In 1652, the American colonists and American Indians signed a peace treaty under it. More than 100 years later, people gathered under the same tree to celebrate the end of the American Revolutionary War. That's why the tulip tree is called the liberty tree. Another tree in this book called the liberty tree is the eastern white pine.

Leaf

The tulip tree **leaf** is **simple** and is shaped something like the outline of a Dutch tulip. It is bright green on top and paler green underneath. In the fall, it turns pale yellow.

Leaf Buds

Samara

Samara Cluster

Flower

The **flower** is **perfect**. That means it has both male and female parts. It has green **petals** with orange splotches at the bottom. Tulip tree flowers appear in late May or early June.

Fruit

The cone-shaped **fruit** is made up of **clusters of samaras**. Each samara holds two **seeds**. When the fruit dries and opens, the samaras scatter, carrying the seeds on the wind.

TUPELO
Nyssa sylvatica
(**niss**-a sill-**vat**-ih-kah)

**Also called
black gum, sour gum,
pepperidge**
Native to eastern U.S.

**Deciduous
30–50 feet tall**

Fall

The tupelo is often found growing in wet ground. The word *tupelo* is an American Indian word meaning "swamp tree." Its **scientific names** are *Nyssa*, referring to the water nymph of Greek mythology, and *sylvatica*, which means "of the woods."

The wood is heavy, tough, and hard to split. It makes strong furniture, boxes, gaskets, broom handles, rolling pins, and ironing boards. American colonists constructed sturdy water pipes out of tupelo wood.

The spongy wood of the **roots** has been used instead of corks to keep large fishing nets from sinking. Bees make honey from tupelo **nectar**. Many kinds of birds and animals eat tupelo **fruit**.

If you chew the end of a tupelo **twig**, it frays (spreads apart) and becomes a little brush. The mountain people from the Alleghenies brushed their teeth with chewed tupelo twigs.

The tupelo is known for its beautiful fall color. But when the weather is very dry, the coloring isn't as spectacular. This is true of many other trees, too.

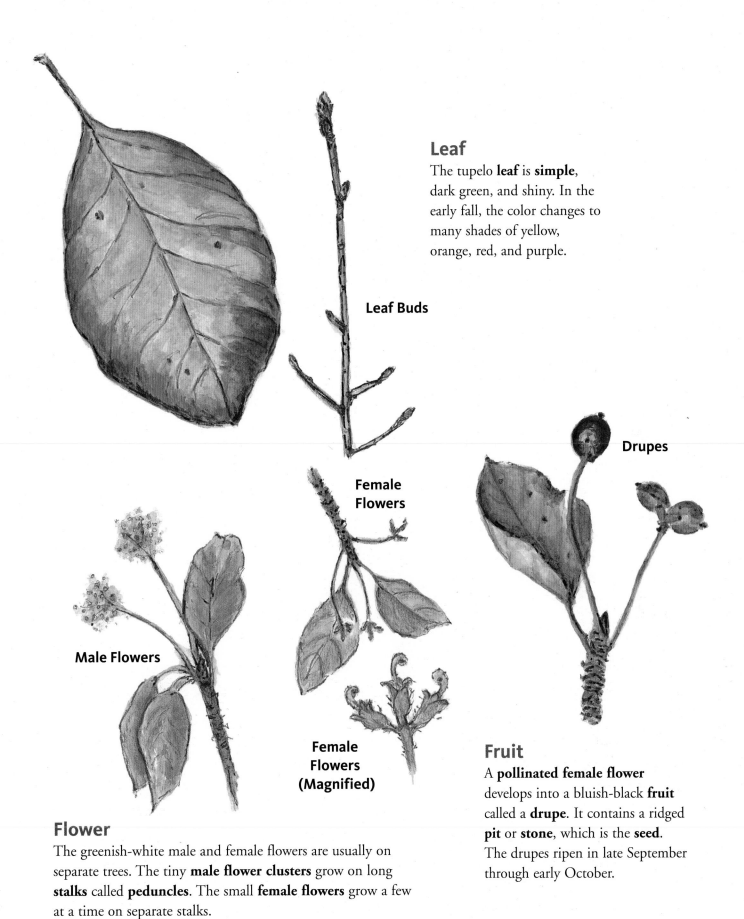

Leaf

The tupelo **leaf** is **simple**, dark green, and shiny. In the early fall, the color changes to many shades of yellow, orange, red, and purple.

Leaf Buds

Drupes

Female Flowers

Male Flowers

Female Flowers (Magnified)

Flower

The greenish-white male and female flowers are usually on separate trees. The tiny **male flower clusters** grow on long **stalks** called **peduncles**. The small **female flowers** grow a few at a time on separate stalks.

Fruit

A **pollinated female flower** develops into a bluish-black **fruit** called a **drupe**. It contains a ridged **pit** or **stone**, which is the **seed**. The drupes ripen in late September through early October.

BLACK WALNUT
Juglans nigra
(**ju**-glans **nye**-grah)

Native to eastern U.S.

Deciduous
70–90 feet tall
State tree
of Ohio

Fall

The black walnut is named for the dark color of the tree's **bark**, wood, and nutshells. It's one of America's most valuable trees. The rich brown wood is made into fine furniture and cabinets. Black walnut wood is so expensive that trees have been stolen right out of the ground. At night, thieves have sneaked into black walnut groves and lifted trees out by helicopter!

Black walnut **shells** are so hard you need a special nutcracker to open them. Instead of whole **nuts**, you usually just get bits and pieces. The tasty nuts are used in cakes and candies. The tough shells are ground up into a gritty powder that cleans and polishes metal, including jet engines.

In the fall, the black walnut is one of the first trees to lose its **leaves**. When the heavy nuts are falling, don't stand under the tree! Squirrels have teeth strong enough to break the shells, and they bury the nuts by the thousands and store them for winter food. In springtime, many black walnut trees sprout from nuts that the squirrels left in the ground. The **roots** produce a substance that is poisonous to some plants. For example, an apple tree can't live near a black walnut tree.

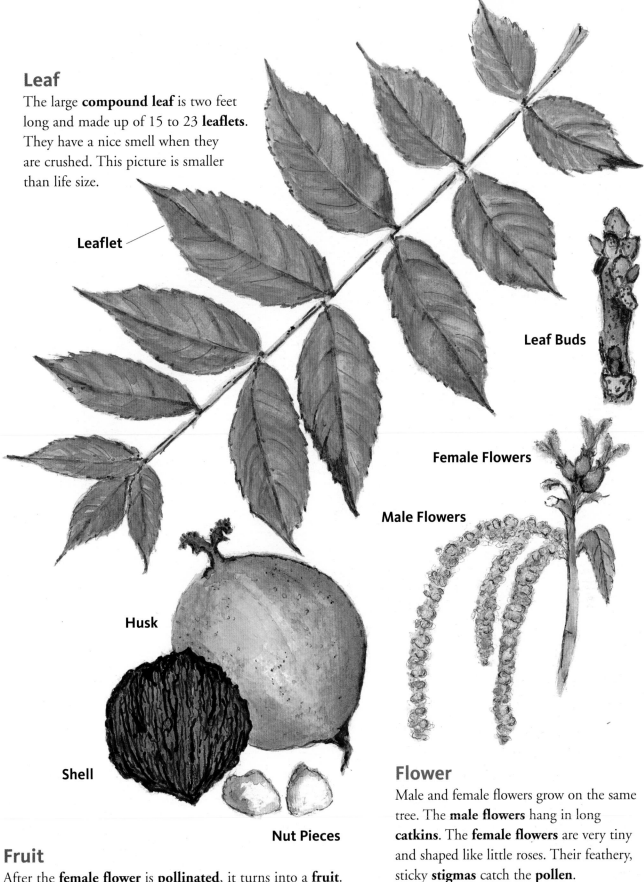

Leaf

The large **compound leaf** is two feet long and made up of 15 to 23 **leaflets**. They have a nice smell when they are crushed. This picture is smaller than life size.

Leaflet

Leaf Buds

Female Flowers

Male Flowers

Husk

Shell

Nut Pieces

Fruit

After the **female flower** is **pollinated**, it turns into a **fruit**. The fruit is a **nut** inside a hard, bony **shell**. The shell is protected by a yellow-green **husk**. The husk drops from the tree and shrivels up. The nutshell is hard to crack open.

Flower

Male and female flowers grow on the same tree. The **male flowers** hang in long **catkins**. The **female flowers** are very tiny and shaped like little roses. Their feathery, sticky **stigmas** catch the **pollen**.

WEEPING WILLOW
Salix x sepulcralis
(**say**-liks ex see-pul-**cray**-lis)

Native to China

Deciduous
30–40 feet tall

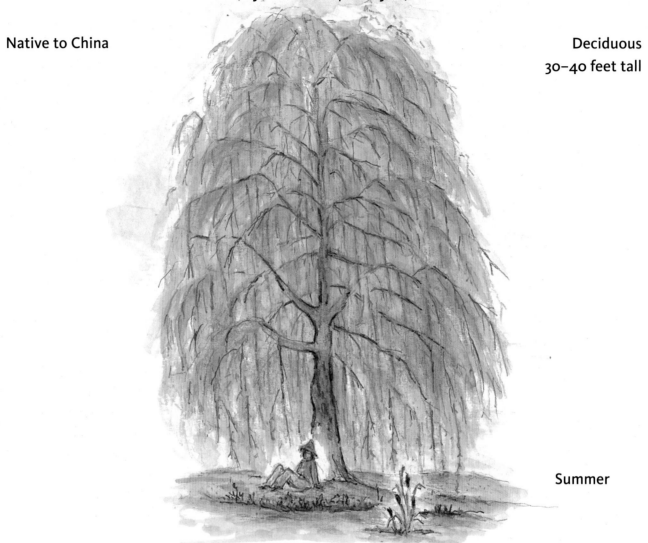

Summer

The weeping willow is native to China. Hundreds of years ago, **cuttings** from the tree were carried along the Chinese trade routes to many places in Asia. Today, this tree is a familiar sight around the world, often alongside rivers and ponds. Its tiny **seeds** easily sprout on the muddy banks. The tree's **weeping habit** makes it easy to identify all year long. There are many **varieties** of weeping willow. They grow fast but don't live to be very old.

A weeping willow needs lots of water and should always be planted near a large natural water supply. If it's not, the **roots** will seek other underground water. They will wrap around wet water pipes and sewer lines and can break the pipes! Wicker furniture and baskets are made from willow. Many kinds of birds nest in the long, weeping branches. The inner bark plays an important part in the area of medicine: It provides an ingredient used in making aspirin.

Napoleon Bonaparte, the emperor of France from 1804 to 1821, was buried under a weeping willow. The weeping willow was supposed to have been his favorite tree.

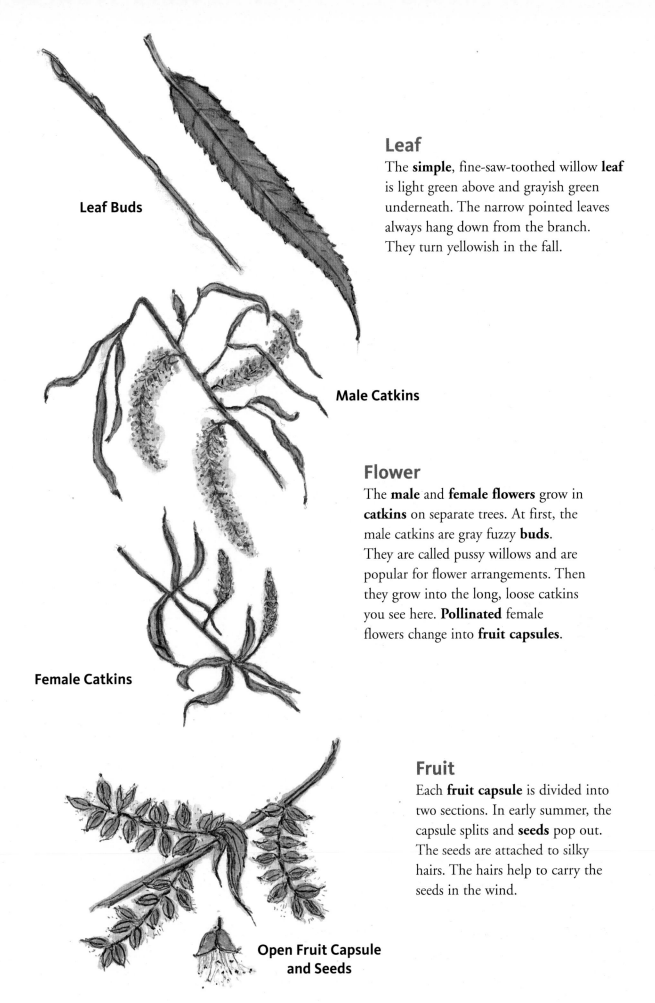

Leaf

Leaf Buds

The **simple**, fine-saw-toothed willow **leaf** is light green above and grayish green underneath. The narrow pointed leaves always hang down from the branch. They turn yellowish in the fall.

Male Catkins

Flower

The **male** and **female flowers** grow in **catkins** on separate trees. At first, the male catkins are gray fuzzy **buds**. They are called pussy willows and are popular for flower arrangements. Then they grow into the long, loose catkins you see here. **Pollinated** female flowers change into **fruit capsules**.

Female Catkins

Fruit

Each **fruit capsule** is divided into two sections. In early summer, the capsule splits and **seeds** pop out. The seeds are attached to silky hairs. The hairs help to carry the seeds in the wind.

**Open Fruit Capsule
and Seeds**

Glossary

acorn — the fruit of an oak tree

alternate leaves — leaves that are staggered on a stem; see **opposite** and **whorled**

annual rings — the rings of wood formed from each year's growth of a tree

anther — the part of a flower that produces pollen

anthocyanins (**an**-tho-**sigh**-a-ninz) — red pigments that are produced by leaves of some trees in the fall

arboretum (ar-buh-**ree**-tum) — a living museum of trees

bark — the protective outer covering of a tree

bast — see **phloem**

blade — the flat, broad part of a leaf

bloom — usually, another word for flower or blossom; it can also mean the whitish, waxy covering on a cone or fruit

blossom — a flower

botanist (**bot**-an-ist) — a scientist who observes and investigates plants

bract — a special kind of leaf that usually forms below a flower or flower cluster

branchlet — a small branch

bud — the part of a plant that will grow into a new stem, leaf, or flower

bur — a prickly seedpod that sticks to fur or clothing

calyx (**kay**-liks) — the sepals of a flower

capsule — a type of dry fruit that contains loose seeds

carbon dioxide — one of the gases that plants use during photosynthesis

carotenoids — (ka-**rot**-en-oidz) orange pigments that exist in some plants

catkin — a long, slim cluster of tiny flowers

cedar apple, **cedar gall** — a round, brown growth on eastern redcedars that makes spores that can cause a fungal disease of apple trees

cedar apple rust — a disease that damages apple leaves and fruit

cellulose — an organic material that makes up cell walls; it is one of the main parts of wood

chlorophyll (**klor**-o-fil) — a green pigment that plants need to trap the sunlight they use for photosynthesis

columnar habit — a description of trees that grow tall and narrow, like columns

common name — a name that people generally use (see **scientific name**)

compound leaf — a leaf made up of more than one leaflet

cone — the part of a conifer that bears pollen or seeds

conifer — a family of trees that bear cones, not flowers; they usually have evergreen needle-shaped leaves

core — see **heartwood**

corolla — the petals of a flower

cross-pollination — when the pollen from one plant fertilizes the flower on another plant to produce seeds

cultivar — a variety or kind of plant that is grown (cultivated) for its special qualities

cutting — a piece of a plant that can grow into an entirely new plant

deciduous (di-**sid**-joo-us) **trees** — trees that drop all their leaves at the same time once a year

drought — a long period of time without rain

drupe — a soft fruit that contains a pit, like a cherry or a peach

dry fruit — a hard fruit, like a nut or a samara

evergreen trees — trees that keep most of their leaves all year

extinct — a species that is no longer alive

fascicle (**fa**-si-kul) — a small cluster, such as a bundle of needles growing from a single point

female flower — a flower that contains a pistil and can produce seeds but not pollen

fertilize — to bring pollen together with an ovule at just the right time to make a seed

filament — the part of the stamen of a flower that holds the anther

fleshy fruit — a soft and juicy fruit, like an apple

flower — the part of a plant that makes pollen and/or seeds and fruit; there are male, female, and perfect flowers

fossil — the impression left in rock of a plant or animal that lived long ago

fruit — the part of a plant that contains and disperses seeds

fungus — a type of organism such as mold and mushrooms that decomposes organic matter

groundwater — underground reserves of water

growth rings — see **annual rings**

gum — see **sap**

habit — the shape in which a plant grows

heartwood — the wood in the center of a tree trunk; it's the oldest wood, and no longer conducts water

husk — see **shell**

hybrid — a plant that is a cross between parents of two different species

immature — not fully developed

invasive — plants that are not native to a particular place and can cause harm, for example, by crowding out native plants

key — see **samara**

knot — a tough area of wood where a branch used to join the trunk

lanceolate (**lan**-see-uh-**late**) **leaf** — a leaf that is shaped like a spear point

leaf, leaves — the part of a plant where most photosynthesis takes place

leaf scar — the mark left on a stem after a leaf falls

leaf stalk — see **petiole**

leaflets — the individual, leaflike parts of a compound leaf

legume — a member of the family of plants that grows long, beanlike seedpods

lenticel (**len**-ti-sel) — a bumpy, spongy spot that forms on bark

male flower — a flower that only releases pollen and does not produce fruit or seeds

mature — adult or fully grown

minerals — inorganic materials found in nature that plants need in order to be healthy, such as nitrogen, phosphorus, and calcium

native — a kind of plant that originated in a certain area

nectar — a sugary liquid found in flowers

needle — a thin, needle-shaped leaf (usually on a conifer)

node — the part of a plant that can grow a new leaf or branch

nut — a type of dry fruit that usually has a hard shell and a softer inner seed

nutlet — a type of dry fruit that has a stony shell around the seed

opposite leaves — leaves that grow in pairs across from each other on a stem

ovary — the part of a flower that bears ovules and develops into the fruit

ovule — a part inside the ovary of a plant that can grow into a seed

oxygen — a gas in the air that plants produce and that most living things need to survive

palmate leaf — a leaf that has "fingers" or divisions radiating from a single base

panicle — a branched cluster of flowers

peduncle — a stalk that connects a flower cluster to the main stem

perfect flower — a flower that contains both male and female parts

petal — one of the often colorful parts of a flower's corolla

petiole (**pet**-ee-ol) — the stalk that attaches a leaf blade to a branch

phloem (**flo**-em) — a layer of wood just inside the bark through which sugars are transported

photosynthesis (**foe**-toe-**sin**-the-sis) — the process by which plants use sunlight trapped by chlorophyll to change carbon dioxide and water into sugars and oxygen

pigment — a chemical that shows as a color

pistil — the female part of a flower, usually made up of the stigma, style, and ovary

pit — a large, hard seed

pitch — see **resin**

pod — a long dry fruit that protects and disperses seeds

pollen — the part of a male flower that is needed for fertilization

pollen cone — a soft cone that releases pollen; also called a male cone

pollination — when pollen lands on a stigma

resin — a thick, sticky liquid produced by conifers

root — the part of the tree that grows mostly underground and holds the tree in place; roots take in water and nutrients

root hairs — the fine extensions of roots that collect water and nutrients from the soil around them

root sap — a liquid that travels through a plant's roots

salts — see **minerals**

samara (suh-**mar**-uh) — a winged dry fruit (see **winged seed**)

sap — the liquid that flows through a plant, carrying sugars and minerals

sapwood — see **xylem**

scale — a hard, woody part of a cone that protects a developing seed

scientific name — a Latinized name chosen by scientists to identify one specific type of plant

seed — a part of a plant in which there is an undeveloped plant along with the food and water that it will use when it begins to grow

seed cone — the part of a conifer that produces scales and seeds; also called a female cone

seedling — a young plant

seedpod — see **pod**

serrated — toothed like a saw

shell — the hard outer case around a seed

simple leaf — a leaf that has one blade

species (**spee**-sees) — a scientific group of plants that can pollinate each other and make seeds

spoon-shaped — a description of oval leaves

spore — a reproductive cell of a mold or fungus

sprout — a shoot and roots produced from a seed

spur shoot — a slow-growing, knobby shoot

stalk — see **stem**

stamen (**stay**-men) — the male part of a flower, including the anther and filament

stem — the aboveground part of a plant, upon which leaves and flowers are attached

stigma — the tip of the female part of a flower upon which pollen lands

stoma, stomata — tiny openings on the underside of a leaf that help it take in and send out gases

stone — see **pit**

stump — the part of a trunk that is left after a tree is cut down

style — in the pistil, the tube that connects the stigma at the top to the ovary at the bottom

sugars — the energy-rich substance that plants produce by photosynthesis

taproot — the large main root of some plants that grows straight down

thorn — a hard branch or twig with a sharp tip

trunk — the main stem of a tree

twig — a small branch

variety — a subgroup of a plant species that grows with a common characteristic

vase-shaped habit — a description of trees that look like containers for flowers

veins — the conducting tubes that carry liquids through a leaf

weeping habit — a description of trees that have trailing, drooping branches

whorled leaves — leaves that grow in a ring around a stem

windbreak — a line of trees planted to block the wind

winged seed — a seed with a papery covering that can be carried by the wind (see **samara**)

xylem (**zie**-lum) — tubular tissue that makes up the rings of wood and conducts water and nutrients

More About Trees

Additional Reading

Ancient Ones: The World of the Old-Growth Douglas Fir
By Barbara Bash
Gibbs Smith, 2002

The Big Tree
By Bruce Hiscock
Boyds Mills Press, 1999

Leaves and Trees (Nature Close Up)
By Elaine Pascoe
Black Birch Press, 2001

Peterson First Guide to Trees
(Peterson Field Guides)
By George A. Petrides
Houghton Mifflin, 1998

Red Leaf, Yellow Leaf
By Lois Ehlert
Harcourt Children's Books, 1991

Tree (DK Eyewitness Books)
By David Burnie
DK Children, 2005

The Tree (First Discovery Books)
By Gallimard Jeunesse and
Pascale De Bourgoing
Cartwheel Books, 1992

A Tree Is Growing
By Arthur Dorros
Scholastic Press, 1997

Trees (Fandex Family Field Guides)
Steven Aronson
Workman, 1998

Winter Tree Finder (Nature Study Guides)
By May T. Watts
Nature Study Guild Publishers, 1970

Web Activities

American Forests
www.americanforests.org
Information and "action opportunities"
to improve the environment with trees

Arbor Day Foundation
www.arborday.org/kids
Educational materials and activities for children
and resources for parents and teachers

Spirit of Trees
www.spiritoftrees.org
Extensive collection of multicultural poems
and folktales about trees, with links to
more resources

Treetures Environmental Education Program
www.treetures.com
Character-driven activities that combine
environmental education and entertainment

More Books for Grown-ups

Fruit Key and Twig Key to Trees and Shrubs
By William M. Harlow
Dover Publications, 1959

Manual of Woody Landscape Plants
Michael A. Dirr
Stipes Publishing, 1998

The Tree: A Natural History of What Trees Are, How They Live, and Why They Matter
By Colin Tudge
Three Rivers Press, 2007

The Tree Identification Book
By George Symonds
Collins, 1973

Index

You can find most of these words on many pages in the book. This index tells you where the words are best explained.

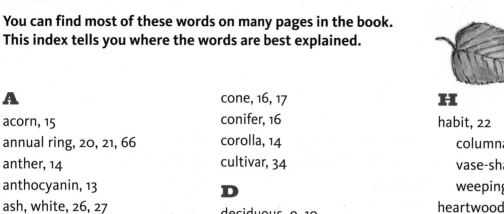

ABOUT THE AUTHOR

Photo: Melissa Balmain Weiner

Gina Ingoglia is the author of more than 80 books for children. She is a graduate of Dickinson College and holds an MA in publishing from New York University. She graduated a George H. Cook Scholar in landscape architecture from Rutgers University and has a private practice in residential landscape and garden design; she is a member of the American Society of Landscape Architects (ASLA). In 1996, she was awarded an honorary doctorate in humanities from Dickinson College. She is vice president of the Brooklyn Botanic Garden Florilegium Society, and her botanical art has been exhibited with the Society in the United States and abroad. From 1987 to 1995 she wrote and illustrated the "Budding Gardener" column for Brooklyn Botanic Garden's publication, *Plants & Gardens News*. She lives in Brooklyn Heights, New York, with her husband, Earl Weiner. They have a son, a daughter, and two grandchildren.

ABOUT BROOKLYN BOTANIC GARDEN

Founded in 1910, Brooklyn Botanic Garden is a 52-acre urban oasis featuring more than 10,000 different kinds of plants from around the world. Along with displaying world-class collections and specialty gardens, Brooklyn Botanic Garden is deeply committed to education, community outreach, and scientific research. The Garden serves as a trusted source of information about horticulture, botany, and the importance of conserving plants and protecting the environment. For more information, visit bbg.org.